A GUIDE TO THE
BRITISH
HOME SERVICE
HELMET
AND ITS BADGES
1878–1914

A GUIDE TO THE BRITISH HOME SERVICE HELMET

AND ITS BADGES

1878–1914

by Ray Westlake

The Naval & Military Press

For Claire, my ever-loving Guide in all things

© Ray Westlake 2020

Published by

The Naval & Military Press Ltd
Unit 5 Riverside
Bellbrook Industrial Estate
Uckfield, East Sussex
TN22 1QQ England

Tel: +44 (0) 1825 749494

www.naval-military-press.com

CONTENTS

Acknowledgments viii

Introduction ix

The Helmet 1

The Helmet Plate 3

The Regiments and Corps 5

Bibliography 112

ACKNOWLEDGMENTS

Images play an important part in this book and I must thank the following who have provided me with many that appear within its pages: The Anne SK Brown Military Collection at Brown University Library and its curator Peter Harrington, Bruce Bassett-Powel and Bob Bennet of the Uniformology website, Coldstream Military Antiques, the Hemswell Antique Centre, Stuart Bates, Garry Gibbs, Major (Retd) Michael Wood TD, Brian Lodge, Benny Bough and Alan Seymour. Without their generous help this 'Guide' would not have been possible. Important to any writer is the support he or she receives at home. My wonderful wife Claire is always there both as a provider of encouragement, and someone who knows where, or not, to put semicolons.

INTRODUCTION

The British Army's Home Service Helmet was introduced in 1878. It was of a German influence and would replace a long line of shakos going back to the days of the Peninsular War and Waterloo. With the new headdress came the helmet plate, those highly desirable items of militaria much sought after today by collectors. Concentrating mainly on the Regular Army, this 'Guide' will describe and illustrate many of those plates. It will, by using contemporary photographs and artwork by leading military artists, also show them being worn. Besides the Regulars, the many hundreds of Victorian and Edwardian Militia, Volunteer and later Territorial Force regiments, would also take into use the home service helmet. But here, as ever, we now tread on a vast and, in most cases, uncharted area of militaria collecting. By including this important aspect of British military history in this book, I will certainly not be in any position to claim completeness. But include it I must, albeit that just the tip of the proverbial iceberg will most likely be reached. Fortunately, and returning to the subject of the Regular Army now, details of the helmet plates worn by officers appear in the several editions of 'Dress Regulations'. I have consulted those for 1883, 1891, 1894, 1900, 1904 and 1911 and from these essential reference works have quoted verbatim. For the helmet plates worn by other ranks, I have turned to old friends, Arthur L Kipling and Hugh King and Volume One of their comprehensive reference work, *Head-dress Badges of the British Army*, referred to in the 'Guide' as 'Kipling and King'.

THE HELMET

Issued by Horse Guards, War Office on 17 May 1883, Dress Regulation for The Officers of the Army, under the heading of 'General Instructions', give the following specification regarding the 'Helmet – Home Pattern':

(a) Cork, covered with blue cloth in four seams, two on each side; peaks front and back, stiffened and covered with cloth without seam; the front peak bound with gilt metal 3/16 inch wide, the back peak with patent leather 1/8 inch wide. Above the peaks and going round the helmet a cloth band ¾ inch wide, and stitched top and bottom. Back peak to centre of crown 10½ inches; front peak to centre of crown 10¼ inches; side to centre of crown 8 inches. Gilt curb-chain chin strap, the links 5/8 inch wide and the strap lined with black velvet. Gilt rose fastenings at the sides; gilt convex bar, ¼ inch wide, down the centre of the back, and to the bottom of the back peak. The bar is in one piece, and is fastened to the helmet by means of two studs and a flattened prolongation of the bar under the back peak. At the top of the helmet, a spike mounted on a cross-piece base.

The dimensions of the spike are—Height of spike from place of insertion in the top of the rose of the cross-piece base 2¾ inches. Total hight of spike and base 3¼ inches. Diameter of spike at point of contact with the top rose of base 7/8 inch.

The cross-piece base is of gilt metal; there is a rose at the top into which the spike is screwed, and a smaller rose on each of the four terminations of the base. A gilt hook at the back of the base, to which the chin strap is attached when not required to be worn under the chin. The width of the base from the point of the front termination to the point of the rear termination, measured in a straight line underneath, 4 and 3/8 inches, that from side to side 3½ inches. The base is attached to the helmet by four screws and nuts. For ventilation, the base is perforated with four holes. A gilt collet is inserted in the crown of the helmet.

(b) In Field Batteries and Garrison Brigades of the Royal Artillery, a gilt ball in a leaf cup is substituted for the spike. Height of ball and cup, 1¾ inches.

(c) In Light Infantry, the helmet is covered with dark green cloth.

(d) In Rifle regiments the helmet is covered with rifle-green cloth, and bronze is substituted for gilt metal in the fittings. Bronze curb-chain chin strap on Morocco leather of the colour of the regimental facings. The leather lined with black velvet.

(e) A description of the plates worn with this pattern of helmet is included in the Dress of the Services for which it is regulation. The plates are also worn on the white pattern helmet at stations for which Puggarees are not authorized.

Regarding section *(b)*, Army Service Corps, medical and veterinary personnel, as well as others in regular contact with horses, would also substitute balls for spikes in their helmets. The thinking here is that a spike could possibly injure a horse as its rider bent down to adjust the girth straps. Infantry officers when mounted also replaced the spike with a ball for the same reason. Green cloth was used for light infantry and rifle regiments, as mentioned in sections *(c)* and *(d)*, and various shades of grey and green by the many volunteer battalions that wore uniforms of those colours.

With their fur caps and bonnets, the Regulars of fusilier and highland regiments did not wear home

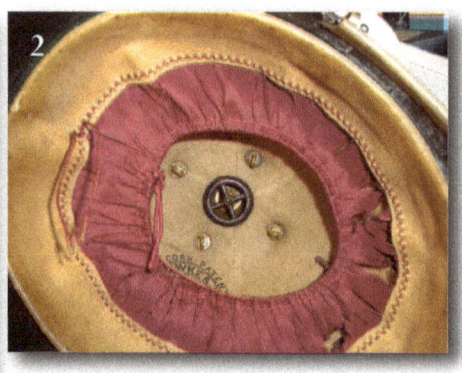

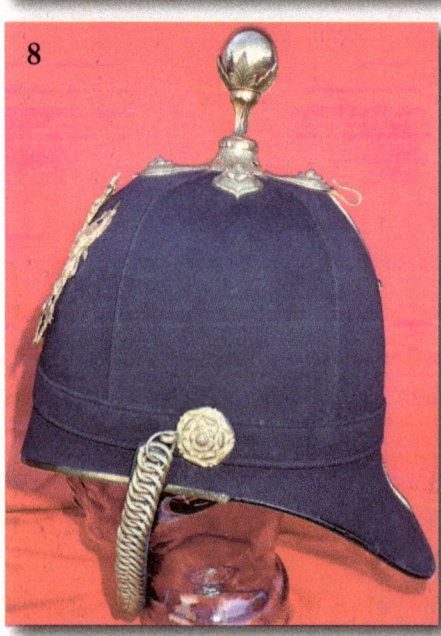

service helmets. Collectors, however, will certainly know of several universal style officers' helmet plates to the latter. These, in fact, were worn of the white foreign service helmet and therefore outside the scope of this book. Rifle regiments favoured the busby after around 1890 and in 1904, both the Royal Scots and King's Own Scottish Borderers would take to the more Scottish in appearance Kilmarnock bonnet.

Illustrations

1 The cross-piece into which the spike or ball is fitted. The chin-strap hook at the rear of the helmet is just visible. (*Stuart Bates*)

2 The inside of the helmet. Clearly seen is the ventilation hole and the four fixing studs that secure the cross-piece to the helmet. (*Stuart Bates*)

3 Another inside view showing how the helmet plate was secured via small strips of soft leather through the lugs.

4 In this side view of an officer's helmet, the chin-strap has been hooked up. (*Stuart Bates*)

5 The hook in its position almost at the top of the helmet and at the commencement of the metal bar that runs down to the back peak. (*JB Military Antiques*)

6 Officers' helmets were transported in tin containers.

7 An example of the spike.

8 An example of the ball fitting, the image also providing clear views of the rear hook and side roses. (*JB Military Antiques*)

THE HELMET PLATE

For details of general pattern helmet plates we find the following in Dress Regulations:

In gilt metal, a star surmounted by the Crown; on the star a laurel wreath; within the wreath a garter inscribed, 'Honi soit qui mal y pense'; within the garter the badge approved for the territorial regiments. On the bottom of the wreath a silver scroll with the designation of the regiment. The dimensions of the plate are—from top of the crown to bottom of plate, back measurement, 5 inches; extreme horizontal width of star, back measurement, 4¼ inches; the bottom central ray of the plate comes halfway over the cloth band of the helmet.

As will be seen, the officers' helmet plate was an elaborate affair made up of several separate pieces. They would appear in their gilts and silver plates, some occasionally turning up bearing hallmarks. Those for other ranks, however, would be much less intricate. What will be described as the 'universal' other ranks back plate would comprise a gilding metal eight-pointed star with the topmost point displaced by a crown. On the star was a laurel wreath which surrounded a voided blank centre. On this would be punched three oblong holes through which would pass the lugs of a detachable, circular centre.

These centres would display the regimental badge, sometimes in white metal, sometimes in both gilding and white metal, and have a shortened version of the title around the edge. At the base of the circle was a spray of laurel. Together with a separate small crown, these helmet plate centres were also used as a glengarry badge. A correct fitting being achieved by placing a blank brass plate inside the cap. This practice was an economy measure by the Government. Helmet plate centres will also be found fitted on the back with an exceptionally long slider. These were used as puggaree badges on foreign service helmets. Other ranks helmet plates for volunteer corps and battalions can be found with their centres permanently fixed.

Under 'Militia Battalions', Dress Regulations note that battle honours must be omitted from badges. In Militia battalions of rifle regiments, the helmets were to have:

A Maltese cross on a red cloth ground…the cross will be bronze, surmounted by a crown, and having a lion at each of its four divisions. In the centre of the cross there will be a bugle, within a circle, bearing the designation of the regiment or battalion. The cross, measured at the back, will be 2½ inches long, and 2½ inches wide.

Illustrations

9 The rear of a king's crown, other ranks helmet plate. Visible are the three (north, east and west) lugs of the centre and the (east and west) lugs that secure the universal plate to the helmet.

10 Backplate used for securing the helmet plate centre and a separate crown to the glengarry cap.

On the subject of battle honours, both the Volunteers and their Territorial Force successors were not allowed to include in their badges those awarded to the Regulars. The Sphinx as a badge was, however, permitted, but the 'Egypt' tablet below was to be left blank. Volunteer service companies would serve alongside the Regulars during the Second Boer War and subsequently 'South Africa' honours with varying dates would appear on helmet plates.

For descriptions of the helmet plates worn by the officers of each regiment, I have quoted verbatim from six editions of Dress Regulations: 1883, 1891, 1894, 1900, 1904 and 1911. The changes are infrequent and minor, but nonetheless important.

THE REGIMENTS AND CORPS

Alexandra, Princess of Wales's Own (Yorkshire Regiment)

Late 19th (1st York North Riding) Princess of Wales's Own Regiment

Dress Regulations, 1883, 1891, 1894, 1900

On Helmet Plates: On a black velvet ground, the Cypher of H.R.H. the Princess of Wales combined with a cross, and surmounted by the Coronet of the Princess. On the centre of the cross, the figures 1875. The Cypher and Coronet in gilt metal; the cross in silver. On the universal scroll 'The Yorkshire Regiment.'

Dress Regulations, 1904

On Helmet Plates: On a black velvet ground, the Cypher of H.R.H. the Princess of Wales combined with a cross, and surmounted by the Coronet of the Princess in silver metal. On the centre of the cross, the figures 1875 and the word Alexandra. On a scroll in silver metal, 'The Princess of Wales's Own Yorkshire Regiment.'

Dress Regulations, 1911

On Helmet Plates: On a black velvet ground, the Cypher of H.R.H. Queen Alexandra as Princess of Wales combined with the Dannebrog, and surmounted by the Coronet of the Princess, in silver metal. On the centre of the cross, the figures '1875' and the word 'Alexandra.' On a scroll in silver metal, 'The Princess of Wales's Own Yorkshire Regiment.' The White Rose in the centre of the scroll.

Illustrations

11 This officer's helmet plate seems to fit in with the 1891 and 1900 Dress Regulations descriptions, save for the cross, etc being in silver. (*Bruce Bassett-Powell and Bob Bennet*)

12 The other ranks helmet plate centre.

13 In this group of officers the chin straps have been hooked up at the rear of the helmet. (*Alan Seymour*)

The White Rose of York is considered an ancient badge of the regiment, the Princess of Wales's Cypher and Coronet being granted when the 19th took on her name in 1875. The pre 1881 officers' helmet plate had a gilt rose on a black leather ground. Below this, the Roman numerals XIX. Also in gilt, 'The Princess of Wales's Own', appeared across the bottom of the star backplate just below the Garter. The post 1881 other ranks helmet plate centres had 'Yorkshire' on the circles and the cypher of Queen Alexandra interlaced with the Dannebrog inscribed '1875' surmounted by a coronet. All in gilding metal.

Army Gymnastic Staff

Star plate with crossed swords in the centre.

Army Ordnance Department

Dress Regulations, 1900, 1904

On Helmet: The Ordnance Arms in silver, on a black velvet ground.

Dress Regulations, 1911

Helmet: Home pattern. Helmet plate, in gilt, an eight-pointed star surmounted by a crown, on the star a laurel wreath; within the wreath the Garter and motto, within the Garter the Ordnance Arms in silver on a black velvet ground.

Kipling and King illustrate and describe an officer's helmet plate on page 262 of their book as follows: 'An eight-pointed star the topmost point displaced by a Victorian crown. On this a laurel wreath. Within the wreath the Garter. In the monogram *AOD*. All in gilt except the monogram which is silver. Black-velvet backing to the centre.' The Ordnance arms type for both officers and other ranks are also illustrated.

Illustration

14 An original watercolour painting by Herbert Benham. (*Anne SK Brown Military Collection, Brown University Library*)

Army Pay Corps

Formation of the Army Pay Corps was notified in Army Order 134 of 1893. Comprising other ranks only, the gilding metal helmet plates were of the crowned star, wreath and Garter

Illustrations

15 All gilding metal helmet plate with detachable 'APC' letters.

16 Gale & Polden postcard. Artist, Ernest Ibbetson, 1909.

pattern with, in the centre, the letters 'APC' on a green cloth ground. Both queen's and king's crown examples exist.

Army Schools

The Corps of Army Schoolmasters was formed by Royal Warrant of 2 July 1846. In Dress Regulations, the helmet plates are listed under the heading of 'Inspectors of Army Schools'.

Dress Regulations, 1891, 1894
Helmet: As for Infantry; gilt plate with 'V.R.' in silver on light blue ground.

Dress Regulations, 1900
Helmet: As for Infantry; in the centre 'V.R.' in silver on light blue ground of copper enamel. No scroll.

Dress Regulations, 1904
Helmet: As for Infantry; in the centre the Royal Cypher in silver, on light blue ground of copper enamel. No scroll.

Dress Regulations, 1911
Helmet: As for Infantry; Within the Garter, the Royal Cypher in gilt on a ground of light blue enamel.

Illustration
17 Helmet plate with Victorian crown. (Bruce Bassett-Powell and Bob Bennett)

Army Service Corps

A most useful article concerning the badges of the Army Service Corps appeared in the August 1963 edition of the *Bulletin of the Military Historical Society*. By Charles Thomas, the item tells how the first Army Service Corps (other ranks only) had been established on 17 December 1869. In 1881 the Commissariat and Transport Staff and ASC merged under the title of Commissariat and Transport Corps. This title in 1888 changing to Army Service Corps.

Dress Regulations, 1883
Under the heading, 'Deputy Assistant Commissary-General' the regulations give: 'Helmet instead of Cocked-Hat—As for Infantry; plate with C.&T.S. in centre on a black ground.

Dress Regulations, 1891, 1894
Helmet Plate: Universal star pattern with 'A.S.C.' in the centre on a black enamelled ground.

Dress Regulations, 1900
Helmet Plate: In silver, the letters 'A.S.C.' in monogram.

Dress Regulations, 1904
Helmet Plate: In silver, the letters 'A.S.C.' in monogram on black enamel.

Dress Regulations, 1911

Helmet Plate: In gilt and eight-pointed star, surmounted by a crown; on the star a laurel wreath; within the wreath the Garter and motto; within the Garter, in silver, the letters 'A.S.C.' in monogram on black enamel.

Writing again in May 1880 (MHS *Bulletin* No 120), Charles Thomas mentions an other ranks helmet plate for the Commissariat and Transport Corps which was a 'Standard gilt plate; on black velvet, 'CTS' in silver, the C and T dotted, the larger S lined.'

Volunteer Infantry Brigade ASC companies had been formed in 1902 and existed until the creation of the Territorial Force in 1908. Kipling and King give two examples of the helmet plates worn. For the Supply Detachment of the Harwich Infantry Volunteer Brigade they give the following description: 'Standard-pattern crown, star and laurel-wreath. Within the wreath a circlet inscribed *Harwich Inf. Vol. Bde. Supply Detachment*. In a voided centre, and in script letters, *SD* on a bar.' The second item is described thus: 'Standard-pattern crown, star and laurel-wreath. Within a circlet inscribed *Sussex & Kent Volr Brigade*. In a voided centre, in script, the letters *ASC*.'

Illustrations

18 Gilt with silver letters helmet plate of the Commissariat and Transport Staff, worn from 1880 to 1888 when it was replaced by the 'ASC' version. (*Bruce Bassett-Powell and Bob Bennet*)

19 An officer's Victorian crown helmet plate with silver letters 'ASC'.

20 Richard Simkin's watercolour painting featuring a mounted officer with, in the background, a trumpeter and waggon team. Note how balls are worn in lieu of spikes. (*Anne SK Brown Military Collection, Brown University Library*)

21 This officer's helmet, with its silver plate and fittings, suggests a Volunteer item. (*Stuart Bates*)

Army Veterinary Corps

The Veterinary Medical Department had been formed in 1858 and this became the Army Veterinary Department in 1881. Made up of other ranks only, the Army Veterinary Corps was established in 1903. Three years later, in 1906, the two were merged to form the Army Veterinary Corps.

Dress Regulations, 1891

Helmet plate: As for Infantry, with 'A.V.D.' on a black ground.

Dress Regulations, 1900

Helmet plate: In silver, on a ground of black enamel, the letters 'A.V.D.' in monogram.

Dress Regulations, 1904

Helmet plate: In silver, on a ground of green enamel, the letters 'A.V.D.' in monogram.

Illustrations

22 A fine specimen of an Army Veterinary Department helmet with silver Victorian crown plate and fittings. (*Stuart Bates*)

23 Officer's gilt helmet plate with silver 'AVD'.

Dress Regulations, 1911

Helmet plate: In gilt, an eight-pointed star surmounted by a crown; on the star a laurel wreath; within the wreath the Garter and motto; within the Garter in silver the letters A.V.C. in monogram on green enamel.

Kipling and King illustrate universal type 'AVC' helmet plates for both officers and other ranks.

Bedfordshire Regiment
Late 16th (Bedfordshire) Regiment

Dress Regulations. 1883

On Helmet Plates: In silver, on a raised ground of blue enamel, an eight-pointed star; on the star, in gilt metal, a Maltese cross. Within a gilt circle on the cross, a Hart in silver crossing a ford. On the universal scroll, 'The Bedfordshire Regt.'

Dress Regulations. 1891, 1894

On Helmet Plates: In silver, on a twisted ground of blue enamel, an eight-pointed star; on the star, in gilt metal, a Maltese cross. Within a gilt circle on the cross, a Hart in silver crossing a ford, the Hart on blue enamel. On the universal scroll, 'The Bedfordshire Regt.'

Dress Regulations. 1900

On Helmet Plates: In silver, on a black velvet ground an eight-pointed star; on the star, in gilt or gilding metal, a Maltese cross. Within a gilt or gilding metal circle on the cross, in silver, a Hart crossing a ford, the Hart on blue enamel. On the universal scroll, 'The Bedfordshire Regt.'

Dress Regulations. 1904, 1911

On Helmet Plates: In silver, on a black velvet ground an eight-pointed star; on the star, in gilt or gilding metal, a Maltese cross. Within a gilt or gilding metal circle on the cross, in silver, a Hart crossing a ford, the Hart on blue enamel. On the universal scroll, 'The Bedfordshire Regiment.'

Major Parkyn notes that a star and cross first appeared as a badge of the regiment about 1830. Early versions of this badge suggest that it is a reproduction of the star of the Order of the Bath with its wavy rays and was possibly adopted as a compliment to William Carr, Viscount Beresford, GCB, GCH who had been appointed colonel of the 16th in 1823. From 1874 until 1881 the Arms of Bedford were used as a collar badge. The Hart was an old badge of the Hertfordshire Militia. The other ranks helmet plate centres had 'Bedfordshire' on the circles and displayed the Maltese Cross on a star with the hart in the centre. All in gilding metal, except the hart which was in white metal.

The Hertfordshire Militia had formed the regiment's 4th Battalion, Kipling and King mentioning a helmet plate with the following description: 'An eight-pointed star, the topmost point displaced by a Victorian crown. On this a laurel-wreath and within the wreath the Garter. In the centre a hart crossing a ford within a scroll inscribed *Hertfordshire*.'

The 1st and 2nd Hertfordshire Rifle Volunteer Corps provided the regiment's 1st and 2nd Volunteer Battalions and helmet plates exist featuring the Hart in the centre. Kipling and King show two examples (Volume One, page 433) both with the wording 'Hertfordshire Rifle Volunteers' on a strap. There is an other ranks version, which the authors describe as being in blackened brass with a white metal Hart, and an officer's Victorian crown pattern which is in white metal with a blue velvet backing.

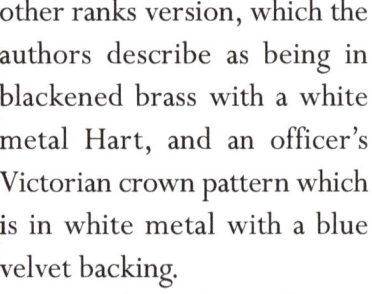

When the Volunteer Force was stood down in 1908, then reinstated as the new Territorial Force, it was the intention to form most of the 1st and 2nd Volunteer

Battalions of the Bedfordshire Regiment (both from Hertfordshire) into a battalion with the title 'Hertfordshire Battalion'. Within months, however, this plan was dropped and instead the former Volunteers provided the Hertfordshire Regiment. An officer's helmet plate has been noted with the title scroll reading 'The Hertfordshire Battalion'. *Hertfordshire Soldiers* by JD Sainsbury includes a photograph of three officers all wearing star plates in 1909.

Illustrations

24 An officers' Victorian crown helmet plate with title scroll reading 'The Bedfordshire Regiment' and gilt and silver centre. (*Bruce Bassett-Powell and Bob Bennet*)

25 In this original watercolour by Harry Payne, the artist has been careful to show the two officers in the Colour Party with gilt metal edging to the front peaks of their helmets. (*Anne SK Brown Military Collection, Brown University Library*)

26 Hertfordshire Rifle Volunteers other ranks helmet plate and an officer's Victorian crown pattern which is in white metal with a blue velvet backing.

27 An officer's helmet with white metal fittings and plate suggesting a possible volunteer item. The regiment had four volunteer battalions, two in Hertfordshire, one from Bedfordshire and another from Huntingdonshire. There is a photograph of a mounted officer of the 1st Volunteer Battalion wearing a grey uniform and helmet with a star plate in Hertfordshire's Soldiers by JD Sainsbury.

28 An other ranks helmet to the 3rd Volunteer Battalion.

Black Watch (Royal Highlanders)

Late 42nd Royal Highland (The Black Watch) and 73rd (Perthshire) Regiments

The Regular battalions of the regiment did not wear the home service helmet. However, the Royal Perthshire Rifles Militia had provided the regiment's 3rd Battalion in 1881, Major HG Parkyn writing in 1948 (Volume 26, *Journal of the Society for Army Historical Research*) recording that the officers' helmet plate for the period prior to that was 'a black metal crowned Star of the Order of the Thistle.'

Illustrations

29 The original uniforms of the 1st Forfarshire Rifle Volunteer Corps were dark grey with black lace worn with dark grey shakos. Scarlet with blue facings and shakos came in 1862, and helmets in 1881. The corps became the 1st (Dundee) Volunteer Battalion Black Watch in 1887.

Illustrated is a detail from a colour plate by Lieutenant-General Sir James Moncrieff Grierson's book, Records of the Scottish Volunteer Force showing a private of the 1st Volunteer Battalion for the period 1904-1908.

30 The 6th Volunteer Battalion Black Watch was formed by the 1st Fifeshire Rifle Volunteer Corps with headquarters at St Andrews, the re-designation coming in 1887. Dark green helmets had been introduced in 1880 and these were worn through to 1908. Illustration from Lieutenant-General Sir James Moncrieff Grierson's book, *Records of the Scottish Volunteer Force*.

31 A fine example of an officer's helmet plate to the 1st Fifeshire Rifle Volunteer Corps.

Border Regiment

Late 34th (Cumberland) and 55th (Westmoreland) Regiments

Dress Regulations, 1883

On Helmet Plate: On a ground of half white, half red enamel, a laurel wreath in silver. Within the wreath, in silver, the Dragon of China, with a scroll above inscribed 'China.' A scroll of special pattern inscribed 'The Border Regiment;' below on another scroll, Arroyo dos Molinos.

Dress Regulations, 1891, 1894

On Helmet Plate: In silver, a laurel wreath; on the wreath a Maltese Cross with a Lion between each division. On the divisions of the Cross, the battles of the regiment. On the centre of the Cross, a raised circle inscribed Arroyo dos Molinos, '1811'. Within the circle a ground of red and white enamel, the Dragon of China in gold on the red enamel and the word 'China' in gold letters on the white. Below the wreath a scroll inscribed 'The Border Regiment.' In the 3rd and 4th Battalions, battles and the word 'China' are omitted.

Dress Regulations, 1900, 1904, 1911

On Helmet Plate: As for Collar [In silver, a laurel wreath; on the wreath a Maltese Cross with a Lion between each division. On the divisions of the Cross, the battles of the regiment. On the centre of the Cross, a raised circle inscribed Arroyo dos Molinos, '1811'. Within the circle, on a ground of red enamel, the Dragon of China in silver and the word 'China' on a silver ground. Below the wreath a scroll inscribed 'The Border Regiment'], but the Dragon and 'China' in gold, and the upper part of the centre filled in with white enamel.

The laurel wreath had been a badge of the 34th Regiment said to commemorate its part in the 1745 Battle of Fontenoy during the War of the Austrian Succession. Then known as Cholmondely's Regiment (General Hon James Cholmondely), the regiment had formed part of the rearguard and played a significant part in foiling an attempt by the French to surround the British forces. Another 34th distinction was the use of a red-and-white tuft in their shakos. This came from the action at Arroyo dos Molinos on 28 October 1811 when the 34th captured their French opposite number—the *34e Regiment d'Infanterie de Ligne*—along with its band and drums. Also from the 34th was the Maltese Cross which, Major HG Parkyn points out, 'Although not officially authorized until 22 July 1881, had figured on the shoulder-belt plates and shakos of the 34th for some years previously.' The Dragon of China recalls the services of the 55th Regiment during the First Opium War of 1841 in which the regiment subsequently saw action at the Battle of Amoy and later during the capture of Chusan.

Kipling and King describe two patterns of pre-1881 officers' helmet plates for the 34th Regiment. Both of universal star design, the first is mentioned as having a black velvet ground on which is displayed a silver laurel wreath. Within that, the number '34'. The second plate, note the authors, showed the number this time on a red and white enamel ground. Below the Garter, a silver scroll inscribed 'Arroyo dos Molinos'. The 55th Regiment is also mentioned, this star plate having the number in the centre, and a silver Dragon of China below the Garter.

Interestingly, an item in the very first edition of *The Bulletin of the Military Historical Society* (1950) mentions an article in the *Journal of the Border Regiment* which notes that the pattern for the new helmet plate had been approved on 22 July 1884. Kipling and King mention that in 1911 the title scroll was altered to read 'The Border Regt.', but there is no indication of this in Dress Regulations.

For other ranks, the helmet plate centres carried the title 'Border' around the circle. Within this,

the Dragon of China within a laurel wreath. Above this, the word 'China'. These plates were all in gilding metal and were worn from 1881 until 1883. The replacement, a white metal version of the central device worn by officers.

The Military Historical Society published a photograph in its May 2016 edition of *The Bulletin* of a helmet plate to the Royal Westmoreland Militia. On a crowned star plate, it had that title on a scroll at the bottom with above, a French style bugle. Within the bugle, the cypher 'VR'. Formed in 1759, the 'Royal' prefix had been granted later, and 'Light Infantry' added to the title in 1854.

In May 2016, the Military Historical Society *(The Bulletin,* No 66) published a photograph of a white metal star plate bearing the title, '1st A Bn. Westmorland Rifle Vols.' on a strap. In the centre, a lion rampant. This battalion had been formed in 1860 and included the several rifle volunteer corps then in existence within the county. In 1880, the 1st Admin Battalion was consolidated as the 1st Westmoreland Rifle Volunteer Corps which in 1887 took on the title of 2nd (Westmorland) Volunteer Battalion of the Border Regiment.

Illustrations

32 An example of the first post-1881 officers' plate with its special title scroll and 'Arroyo dos Molinos' honour below the Garter. *(Bruce Bassett-Powell and Bob Bennet)*

33 The new plate, first mentioned in the 1891 Dress Regulations, the wreath now around the addition of a Maltese Cross and the honour, now with its date, on a circle. (*Bruce Bassett-Powell and Bob Bennet*)

34 An other ranks post-1883 helmet plate.

35 An original watercolour painting by Harry Payne who shows a corporal wearing both the Queen's and King's Medals for South Africa. (*Anne SK Brown Military Collection, Brown University Library*)

36 With the 'Arroyo dos Molinos 1811' honour removed, and its place taken by 'Honi soit qui mal y pense'. 'China' and all other battles omitted, the helmet shown was worn by one or other of the regiment's volunteer battalions.

37 The other ranks helmet plate to the 1st Volunteer Battalion with its additional title scroll.

38 King's crown officers' helmet plate. (*Brian Lodge*)

Buffs (East Kent Regiment)
Late 3rd (East Kent) Regiment (The Buffs)

Dress Regulations, 1883, 1891, 1894

On Helmet Plates: On a black velvet ground, the Dragon in silver. On the universal scroll, 'The East Kent Regiment.'

Dress Regulations, 1900, 1904, 1911

On Helmet Plates: On a black velvet ground, the Dragon in silver. On the universal scroll, 'The East Kent Regiment.' Above the Garter a scroll inscribed 'The Buffs.'

As is the case with many ancient regimental badges, the origins of that belonging to the Buffs is obscure. The Green Dragon was mentioned in the Clothing Regulations of 1747 and in the Royal Warrant of 1751 where it is described as the ancient badge. Major HG Parkyn writing in his book *(Military) Shoulder-Belt Plates and Buttons* suggests that the badge probably traces back to the fact that the regiment was raised from the Trained Bands of the City of London. The 'Square Mile', of course, features a dragon in its arms, but it is silver, and the green variety used by the Buffs has no cross of St George on its wings. The beast also has a connection with Ghent and regimental historian Richard Cannon suggests that the dragon was possibly placed on the Colours when the Buffs were stationed at the Belgium city in 1707.

Wearing dark green uniforms with scarlet facings, the 2nd Kent (East Kent) Rifle Volunteer Corps under General Order 63 of May 1883 was re-designated as 1st Volunteer Battalion Buffs (East Kent Regiment). Helmets were worn with Maltese Cross plates, the centres having the White Horse and motto *Invicta* from the arms of Kent on a red cloth backing.

Illustrations

39 The Dragon featured in the centre of the regiment's officers' helmet plates. We see it here in illustration (39), the single silver title scroll having 'The East Kent Regiment'. (*Bruce Bassett-Powell, Bob Bennet*)

40 In 1900 a change was made to the officers' helmet plates which saw an additional scroll inscribed 'The Buffs' placed just below the crown. About this time a change was also made to the centres of the other ranks helmet plates which also featured the Dragon. The original title wording on the circle was 'East Kent', but a new version had the much lengthier 'The Buffs East Kent Regiment' which made necessary the shortening of the usual laurel sprays so as to make room.

41 A photograph taken by Gregory & Co of the Strand showing a group of five bandsmen all wearing Victorian crown plates on their blue helmets.

42 As a party from the regiment stand at ease in the distance, a sergeant reports to his officer in this watercolour by Harry Payne. Note how the artist has been careful to shown how the officer's helmet has a gilt metal edging to the peak. (*Anne SK Brown Military Collection, Brown University Library*)

43 The image of a trombonist is from WJ Gordon's Bands of the British Army, the artwork being by Frederick Stansell.

44 From Richard Simkin, a study of three members of the regiment (an officer in the centre). The watercolour was produced as a supplement to the Army and Navy Gazette and published on 4 April 1891.

45 Another image from Gregory & Co showing two sergeants from the regiment.

Cameronians (Scottish Rifles)

Late 26th (Cameronians) and 90th (Perthshire Volunteers) (Light Infantry) Regiments

Dress Regulations, 1883, 1891, 1894

On Helmet Plates: A thistle wreath surmounted by a crown. On the leaves of the wreath, the battles of the regiment. Within the wreath, a mullet, and below the mullet, a bugle with strings. On a tablet to the right of the wreath, the Dragon of China; on a tablet to the left, the Sphinx. On the bottom of the wreath, a scroll inscribed 'The Scottish Rifles.'

The regiment had ceased to war the helmet in 1892. The badges of the 26th Regiment featured a Dragon superscribed 'China' and, from the crest of the Douglas family, a mullet star. Bugle-horn badges were worn by the 90th, the Sphinx superscribed 'Egypt' being authorised for both regiments in July 1802. For the 26th Regiment, the officers' helmet plates were of a gilt star pattern and featured the device of a silver mullet on a black velvet ground. The numeral '26' was placed below the crown in the space where the top of the wreath meets. The name 'Cameronians' was inscribed on a scroll below the Garter. Both the numeral and scroll were silver.

The Cameronians had five volunteer battalions. The 1st Lanarkshire Rifle Volunteer Corps served without change of title as the 1st. Headquarters were in Glasgow and grey helmets with bronze Maltese Cross plates were taken into use in 1878. Both the 2nd and 3rd Volunteer Battalions wore blue helmets with silver or white metal fittings. From Hamilton, the 2nd had replaced their glengarry caps with helmets for full dress wear in 1881. General Grierson notes that on 6 May 1902 the battalion was authorised to wear as its sole uniform a drab service dress, the officers at the same time having the uniform of the regulars as its full dress. The 3rd Lanarkshire Rifle Volunteer Corps provided the regiment's 3rd Volunteer Battalion, their shakos being replaced by helmets in March 1878. The 4th Lanarkshire Rifle Volunteer Corps had replaced their shakos with helmets in 1878. As 4th Volunteer Battalion Cameronians from 1887, the helmet was worn until April 1904 when a drab service dress with scarlet piping on the trousers became the sole uniform. The officers, however, continued to wear the uniform of the regulars in full dress. With headquarters at Airdrie, the 7th Lanarkshire Rifle Volunteer Corps in March 1879 changed its uniform to scarlet tunics with yellow facings, worn with blue helmets. Re-designation as 5th Volunteer Battalion was ordered in 1887 and disbandment as such took place with effect from 1 April 1897.

Major HG Parkyn refers to an officer's helmet plate worn by the 2nd Royal Lanarkshire Militia (Volume 26, 1948, of the *Journal of the Society for Army Historical Research*) as follows, 'A spray of three thistles in silver on a black velvet ground, all within a circle inscribed "2nd Royal Lanark Militia." A scroll below the circle inscribed

"Nemo me impune lacessit." The whole on a star of the Order of the Thistle and superimposed on a crowned star of eight points.' The 2nd Lanarkshire Militia had provided the regiment's 3rd and 4th Battalions in 1881.

Illustrations

46 Officer's helmet to the 26th Regiment. (*Benny Bough*)

47 By Richard Simkin, a piper and private in 1879.

48 Colour plate by Richard Simkin featuring a pioneer, drum major and drummer.

49 Colour plate by Richard Simkin showing a bandsman and officers wearing the white foreign service helmet.

50 The post-1881 officers; helmet plate. (*Bruce Bassett-Powell and Bob Bennet*)

51 Artist Orlando Norie (1832-1901) painted the regiment in 1882, the scene showing a tented camp in the background and featuring five members of the regiment, including a mounted officer. (*Anne SK Brown Military Collection, Brown University Library*)

52 Grey officers' helmet to the 1st Lanarkshire Rifle Volunteer Corps with Maltese Cross plate. (*Benny Bough*)

53 Detail from one of the colour plates used in Lieutenant-General Sir James Moncrieff Grierson's book, Records of the Scottish Volunteer Force 1859-1908 showing two members of the 1st Lanarkshire Rifle Volunteer Corps.

54 Colour plate illustrating the several uniforms worn by the 2nd Volunteer Battalion and 3rd Lanarkshire Rifle Volunteer Corps From Lieutenant-General Sir James Moncrieff Grierson's book, Records of the Scottish Volunteer Force 1859-1908.

55 Private of the 7th Lanarkshire Rifle Volunteer Corps, later 5th Volunteer Battalion.

Cheshire Regiment

Late 22nd (Cheshire) Regiment

Dress Regulations, 1883

On Helmet Plates: In silver, on a black velvet ground, an eight-pointed star. Within a gilt circle on the star, the Prince of Wales's Plume on a burnished silver ground. On the universal scroll 'The Cheshire Regiment.'

Dress Regulations, 1891

On Helmet Plates: In silver, on a black velvet ground, an eight-pointed star. Within a gilt circle on the star, the Prince of Wales's Plume on a burnished silver ground. The plume in silver, the coronet in gilt or gilding metal. On the universal scroll 'The Cheshire Regiment.'

Dress Regulations, 1894

On Helmet Plates: In silver, on a black velvet ground, an eight-pointed star. Within a gilt circle on the star, the Prince of Wales's Plume on a burnished silver ground. On the universal scroll 'The Cheshire Regiment.'

Dress Regulations, 1900, 1904, 1911

On Helmet Plates: In silver, on a black velvet ground, an eight-pointed star. Within a gilt or gilding metal circle on the star, the Prince of Wales's Plume on a burnished silver ground. The plume in silver, the coronet in gilt or gilding metal. On the universal scroll 'The Cheshire Regiment.'

The other ranks helmet plate centres also had the Prince of Wales's Plumes, coronet and motto, all in gilding metal except the plumes which were in white metal. The Prince of Wales's device had been an old badge of the Cheshire Militia and was taken into use by the Cheshire Regiment in 1881. Major HG Parkyn, in an article published by the Society for Army Historical Research (*The Journal*, Vol 15, 1936), noted how the device was worn on the helmet plates with a red cloth backing and within a circle inscribed with the title of the regiment.

Illustrations

56 An officers' Victorian crown helmet plate with the gilt coronet as mentioned for the first time in Dress Regulations 1900. (*Bruce Bassett-Powell and Bob Bennet*)

57 Edgar Holloway's original artwork for one of Gale & Polden's military postcard sets. The artist has shown the drum major and drummers wearing king's crown helmet plates. (*Anne SK Brown Military Collection, Brown University Library*)

58 Consolidation of the several administrative battalions of Cheshire rifle volunteer corps in 1880 saw five battalions formed—the 1st to 5th Cheshire Rifle Volunteer Corps. These, in 1887 would be re-designated as 1st to 5th Volunteer Battalions of the Cheshire Regiment. An officer's grey cloth helmet to the 1st Cheshire Rifle Volunteer Corps is illustrated. The central device is from the arms of the Earl of Chester.

Connaught Rangers
Late 88th (Connaught Rangers) and 94th Regiments

Dress Regulations, 1883, 1891, 1894

On Helmet Plates: In silver, on a dark green velvet ground, the Harp with scroll, inscribed Quis separabit. A sprig of laurel issues from either end of the scroll. On the universal scroll, 'The Connaught Rangers.'

Dress Regulations, 1900

On Helmet Plates: In silver, on a black velvet ground, the Harp with scroll, inscribed Quis separabit. A sprig of laurel issues from either end of the scroll. On the universal scroll, 'The Connaught Rangers.'

Dress Regulations, 1904, 1911

On Helmet Plates: In silver, on a dark green velvet ground, the Harp with scroll, inscribed Quis separabit. A sprig of laurel issues from either end of the scroll. On the universal scroll, 'The Connaught Rangers.'

Major HG Parkyn in his book *(Military) Shoulder-Belt Plates and Buttons,* notes how the Harp and Crown, together with the motto *Quis separabit*, was an old badge of the 88th Regiment, having been authorized on 23 December 1830. The officers' pre-1881 helmet to the 88th showed the Harp and '88' in the centre with, below the Garter on a scroll, the *Quis separabit* motto. Kipling and King record for the 94th Regiment, an officers' plate with the numeral on a black velvet ground with, below the Garter, a silver elephant. Major Parkyn notes that this badge had been originally authorized in 1807 with the honour 'Seringapatam' to a former 94th Regiment that had been disbanded in 1818.

Illustrations

59 Officers' Victorian crown helmet plate. (*Bruce Bassett-Powell and Bob Bennet*)

60 An other ranks gilding metal helmet plate with Victorian crown. Kipling and

King show two versions of the other ranks helmet plate centre. Their item No 352 is the one illustrated here, but a variation, which has a much slimmer Harp, they show at 351.

61 A plate from Lieutenant-Colonel HFN Jourdain and Edward Fraser's history of the Connaught Rangers. Two helmet plates are shown, the other ranks pattern having the large Harp centre. The regiment was disbanded in 1922.

62 An original watercolour painting by Harry Payne showing two members of the regiment in conversation. Both wear home service helmets with king's crown plates and silver elephant badges on their collars. (*Anne SK Brown Military Collection, Brown University Library*)

63 Richard Simkin's Supplement No 102 from his 'Military Types' series for the Army and Navy Gazette. Published on 6 June 1896, the image features three officers, one holding a King's Colour.

64 A bandsmen from WJ Gordon's Bands of the British Army, artwork by Frederick Stansell.

Devonshire Regiment

Late 11th (North Devon) Regiment

Dress Regulation, 1883, 1891, 1894, 1900, 1904, 1911

    On Helmet Plates: The Castle of Exeter, with scroll inscribed Semper fidelis, in silver, on a black velvet ground. On the universal scroll 'The Devonshire Regt.'

The Castle of Exeter and the motto *Semper fidelis* (Ever faithful) was a badge of the old Devon Militia adopted by the Devonshire Regiment in 1881.

Pre 1881 officers' helmet plate centres displayed just the number '11' on a black velvet ground.

Illustrations

65 Officers' helmet plate with silver title scroll reading 'The Devonshire Regiment', a shortened 'Regt' version appearing sometime before 1900. (*Bruce Bassett-Powell and Bob Bennet*)

66 An example of an officer's helmet with the title 'Regiment' in full on display at the Bygones Museum in Fore Street, St Marychurch, Torquay.

67 Other ranks, all brass helmet plate centres also displayed the Exeter Castle with 'Devonshire' on the circle.

68 Harry Payne's original watercolour painting shows two drummers standing chatting in the background. Both have their helmet chin straps hooked up, one wearing the Queen's and King's Medals awarded for service in the Second Boer War. With strap placed firmly under his chin, this time, a private stands at ease. (*Anne SK Brown Military Collection, Brown University Library*)

69 On display at the Bygones Museum in St Marychurch, Torquay an officer's helmet of the 3rd Volunteer Battalion.

70 Officers' helmet for the 5th (Haytor) Volunteer Battalion with its rampant lion center piece.

71 Other ranks helmet, 5th (Haytor) Volunteer Battalion.

72 An other ranks helmet plate shown to the 4th Volunteer Battalion.

Dorsetshire Regiment

Late 39th (Dorsetshire) and 54th (West Norfolk) Regiments

Dress Regulations, 1883, 1891, 1894, 1900, 1904, 1911

    On Helmet Plates: In silver, on a black velvet ground, the Castle and Key. A scroll above the Castle inscribed Primus in Indis, and one below, inscribed Montis insignia Calpe. On the universal scroll 'The Dorsetshire Regiment.'

The Castle, Key and motto of Gibraltar, *Montis insignia Calpe* (Badge of the Rock of Gibraltar) were authorized as a badge in commemoration of the 39th Regiment's services during the great siege of 1779-83. Also used on insignia was the motto *Primus in Indis* (First in India) which recognises that the 39th was the first British regiment of the Line to serve in India. Other ranks helmet plate centres had the Caste and Key with a scroll inscribed 'Gibraltar' above, and another below with the words '*Primus in Indis*'. All in gilding metal, the circles had 'Dorsetshire'. Examples exist with both two- and three-towered castles.

Illustrations

73 Painting of the 39th Regiment by Orlando Norie showing several officers observing the men firing. (*Anne SK Brown Military Collection, Brown University Library*)

74 The two-towered Gibraltar Castle officer's helmet plate.

75 King's crown officer's helmet with three towers plate.

76 A Harry Payne's original watercolour featuring a sergeant with a king's crown helmet plate.

77 Officer's helmet plate to the Dorsetshire Militia which has in the centre of a universal plate a stork below a coronet. This device is the crest of Lord Rivers who, as the Hon George Pitt, raised the Dorsetshire Militia in 1759. (*Gary Gibbs*)

78 Maltese Cross type helmet plate to the Dorsetshire Rifle Volunteers which has a bugle-horn in the centre of a circle inscribed 'Pro Patria'. The four arms of the cross are inscribed too. On the top arm, the word 'Dorset', the left arm has 'Rifle', and the right, 'Volrs.' The bottom arm has a fasces (a bundle of rods bound around an axe), that ancient Roman symbol of power and unity. (*Gary Gibbs*)

Duke of Cambridge's Own (Middlesex Regiment)

Late 57th (West Middlesex) and 77th (East Middlesex) (or Duke of Cambridge's Own) Regiments

Dress Regulations, 1883, 1891, 1894, 1900, 1904

On Helmet Plates: In silver, on a black velvet ground, a laurel wreath; within the wreath, the Prince of Wales's Plume; below the Plume, the Coronet and Cypher of H.R.H. the Duke of Cambridge. On the bottom of the wreath a scroll inscribed 'Albuhera.' On the universal scroll 'The Middlesex Regt.'

Dress Regulations, 1911

On Helmet Plates: In silver, on a black velvet ground, a laurel wreath; within the wreath, the Prince of Wales's Plume;

below the Plume, the Coronet and Cypher of H.R.H. the late Duke of Cambridge. On the bottom of the wreath a scroll inscribed 'Albuhera'. On the universal scroll 'The Middlesex Regt'. Note: The Duke of Cambridge had died in 1904.

The Prince of Wales's plumes, coronet and motto had been granted as a badge to the 77th Regiment in 1876. The battle honour 'Albuhera' commemorates the outstanding gallantry of the 57th Regiment at Albuhera during the Peninsular War. Kipling and King describe the pre-1881 officer's helmet plate as having the numerals '57' on a black velvet ground and the post-1881 other ranks helmet plate centre as: 'On circlet: *Middlesex*. In centre: Within a laurel-wreath, the Cypher and Coronet of the Duke of Cambridge surmounted by the Prince of Wales's plumes, coronet and motto. At the foot, a scroll inscribed *Albuhera*. The Prince of Wales's plumes, coronet and motto in white-metal, remainder in gilding metal.'

Illustrations
79 Officer's Victorian crown helmet plate. (*Bruce Bassett-Powell and Bob Bennet*)

80 Officer's king's crown helmet plate. (*Brian Lodge*)

81 Other ranks helmet plate centre with fitted long slider for use on a puggaree.

82 An original watercolour painting by Harry Payne featuring a lance-corporal wearing a king's crown helmet plate.

(Anne SK Brown Military Collection, Brown University Library)

83 Supplement No 89 from Richard Simkin's 'Military Types' series. Produced for the Army and Navy Gazette, the print was published on 4 May 1895.

84 A Gale & Polden postcard featuring the Drums. Artwork by Ernest Ibbetson.

85 The 3rd Middlesex Rifle Volunteer Corps originated in 1860. It became a volunteer battalion of the Middlesex Regiment in 1881, being re-designated as 1st Volunteer Battalion in 1898. This colour plate featuring three officers of the battalion was published in Records of The Third Middlesex Rifle Volunteers, published in 1885 by Simpkin, Marshall & Co of London. The book is by ET Evans who also provided the artwork. The helmet plate was of the Maltese Cross type with a bugle in the centre of a circle inscribed 'Third Middlesex Rifle Volunteers'.

86 A private in marching order from Records of The Third Middlesex Rifle Volunteers by ET Evans.

87 Stretcher bearers of the 17th Middlesex (North Middlesex) Rifle Volunteer Corps. With headquarters in Camden Town, this corps served as a volunteer battalion of the Middlesex Regiment, transferring to the Territorial Force in 1908 as the 19th London Regiment. Note how balls have replaced the helmet spikes.

88 Other ranks king's crown helmet plate, 2nd Volunteer Battalion. Note the absence of the 'Albuhera' scroll. *(Brian Lodge)*

89 Other ranks queen's crown helmet plate, 2nd Volunteer Battalion. Note the absence of the 'Albuhera' scroll. *(Brian Lodge)*

90 Officer's Victorian crown helmet plate with blank 'Albuhera' scroll. , 1st Volunteer Battalion. *(Brian Lodge)*

91 Officer's helmet plate with king's crown and blank 'Albuhera' scroll. *(Brian Lodge)*

92 Officer's helmet plate with king's crown and no 'Albuhera' scroll. *(Brian Lodge)*

Duke of Cornwall's Light Infantry

Late 32nd (Cornwall) Light Infantry and 46th (South Devonshire) Regiments

Dress Regulations, 1883, 1891, 1894

On Helmet Plate: In gilt metal, on a ground of dark green velvet, a bugle with strings. On the strings of the bugle two red feathers set in gilt metal. On the stems of the feathers, in silver, a turreted archway. On the universal scroll, 'The Duke of Cornwall's Lt. Infy.'

Dress Regulations, 1900, 1904, 1911

On Helmet Plate: In gilt or gilding metal, on a ground of dark green velvet, a bugle with strings. On the strings of the bugle two red feathers set in gilt or gilding metal. On the stems of the feathers, in silver, a turreted archway. On the universal scroll, 'The Duke of Cornwall's Lt. Infy.'

The bugle horn was adopted by the 32nd Regiment in 1858, the 'Light Infantry' title having been given as a distinction for the gallantry shown by it throughout the defence of the residency at Lucknow during the

Indian Mutiny. Adopted as a collar badge in 1876 was the coronet of the Duke of Cornwall together with the fifteen bezants from the county arms and the motto One and All. Two red feathers, a badge distinction of the 46th, dates from the American War of 1777 when, after inflicting heavy casualties on the opposing side, the American battalion concerned vowed to take revenge the next day. In defiance, the 46th dyed their white feather red so as they could be easily recognised. The turreted archway dates from 1881 and is a representation of the ancient gateway to Launceston Castle, a device used on the Great Seal of the Duke of Cornwall.

Kipling and King describe the officers' pre-1881 helmet plate for the 32nd Regiment as: 'A strung bugle-horn with the Roman numerals *XXXII* within the strings on a green-velvet ground, all within the Garter in gilt superimposed on a silver star 2.54" high by 2-34" wide. The rays of the star have beaded edges. All within the standard gilt laurel-wreath.' For the same period, the 46th Regiment plate had the numerals in gilt on a black velvet ground. Regarding an other ranks plate for the 32nd, D Endean Ivall and Charles Thomas in their authorative book, *Military Insignia of Cornwall*, note that it may never have existed and that the plates from the old shako plate could have been used on the helmets.

The post-1881 other ranks helmet plate centre is described by Kipling and King as follows: 'On circlet: *Duke of Cornwall's Light Infantry*. In centre: A Bugle with strings, upon which is superimposed a castle. Behind the castle two feathers in saltire. All in gilding-metal.' Due to the length of the title, the usual sprig of laurel was omitted. D Endean Ivall and Charles Thomas illustrate an other ranks helmet plate and an example of how the centre was used together with a separate crown as the glengarry badge. King's crown versions of both the officers and other ranks helmet plates also appear in *Military Insignia of Cornwall*.

The Duke of Cornwall's Light Infantry had two volunteer battalions, the 1st with headquarters at Falmouth, moving to Truro in 1902, and the 2nd which was at Bodmin. These had been formed, respectively, by the 1st and 2nd Cornwall Rifle Volunteer Corps, the re-designation coming in 1885. In 1966, Charles Thomas wrote an interesting article for the Military Historical Society (*The Bulletin,* No 66) in which he mentioned that the 1st Volunteer Battalion adopted a very dark grey helmet about 1882-3 which bore a black Maltese Cross plate. Mounted in the center, in white metal, was the shield charged with the fifteen bezants from the Cornwall arms with, below, the motto 'One and All'. This plate, notes Charles Thomas, was worn unchanged until 1908. A sketch of this item appeared in *Military Insignia of Cornwall* by D Endean Ivall and Charles Thomas.

Illustrations

93 The officers' Victorian crown helmet plate. (*Bruce Bassett-Powell and Bob Bennet*)

94 Other ranks helmet plate centre. Note how the usual sprig of laurel at the bottom of the circle has been removed so as to make room for the title.

95 The original artwork supplied by artist Harry Payne for a postcard. It features an officer who wears both the Queen's and King's Medals for South Africa. (*Anne SK Brown Military Collection, Brown University Library*)

96 From The British Army and Auxiliary Forces by Colonel C Cooper-King, a photograph by Gregory of the Strand featuring a sergeant wearing the Indian General Service Medal and Kadieves Star.

97 Richard Simkin's Supplement No 69 in his 'Types of the British Army' series. The scene shows a party from the regiment on a exercise, the artist being careful to show the metal bar at the back of the officer's helmet. Produced for the Army and Navy Gazette, the print was published on 2 September 1893.

98, 99 In the late D Endean Ivall and Charles Thomas's most valuable book, we find sketches of two pre-1885 helmet plates for the 2nd Volunteer Battalion: that for officers (6) and other ranks (7). The post-1885 officers' plates were as for the regulars, but in silver with black velvet centre backing and no red behind the feathers. The additional scroll read '2nd Volunteer Battalion'.

Duke of Edinburgh's (Wiltshire Regiment)

Late 62nd (The Wiltshire) and 99th (The Duke of Edinburgh's) Regiments

Dress Regulations, 1883, 1891, 1894

On Helmet Plates: On a black velvet ground, the Maltese Cross in lined gilt metal, with burnished edges. On the cross, a round convex, burnished plate. On the plate, in silver, the Cypher surmounted by the Coronet. On the universal scroll. 'The Wiltshire Regiment.'

Dress Regulations, 1900, 1904, 1911

On Helmet Plates: On a black velvet ground, the Maltese Cross in lined gilt or gilding metal, with burnished edges. On the cross, a round convex burnished plate. On the plate, in silver, the Cypher surmounted by the Coronet. On the universal scroll. 'The Wiltshire Regiment.'

The name of the Duke of Edinburgh was first linked with the title of the 99th Regiment in 1874. The Maltese Cross was an old badge of the 62nd. Both the cross and the Duke's cypher would appear on the post-1881 officers' helmet plates, the other ranks having the same devices on the helmet plate centres which had 'Wiltshire' on the circle.

Illustrations

100 Officer's Victorian crown helmet plate. (*Bruce Bassett-Powell and Bob Bennet*)

101 A regimental sergeant major addresses a private in this original watercolour painting by Harry Payne. (*Anne SK Brown Military Collection, Brown University Library*)

102 Devises Station, and a party from the Wiltshire Regiment await a train in artist Richard Simkin's Supplement No 91 from his 'Military Types' series. Issued with the Army and Navy Gazette, the print was published on 6 July 1895.

Duke of Wellington's (West Riding Regiment)

Late 33rd (The Duke of Wellington's) and 76th Regiments

Dress Regulations, 1883, 1891, 1894, 1900, 1904, 1911

On Helmet Plate: In silver, on a black velvet ground, the Crest of the Duke of Wellington, with motto on a scroll below, Virtutis fortuna comes. On the universal scroll 'The West Riding Regiment.'

With the 1853 title came the Duke's crest and motto, *Virtutis fortuna comes* (Fortune accompanies honour) as a badge for the 33rd. The regiment's first officers' helmet plate is described by Kipling and King as follows: On a black velvet ground a circlet inscribed with the motto of the Duke of Wellington, *Virtutis fortuna comes* and within this his crest viz: Out of a ducal coronet a demi-lion rampant holding a forked pennon flowing to the sinister one third per pale from the staff charged with the Cross of St George. At the junction of the laurel-wreath the numerals *33*. All in silver. A plate for the 76th Regiment has also been noted which has an elephant with howdah above the numerals on a black velvet ground, all in silver. The elephant and howdah had been conferred of the 76th Regiment in January 1807 to commemorate its long and distinguished service in India during the years 1788 to 1806.

The other ranks helmet plate centre had the Duke's crest and 'West Riding' on the circle.

The reorganisations of 1881 saw the 6th West York Militia re-designated as 3rd and 4th Battalions Duke of Wellington's Regiment. In August 1974 (*The Bulletin* No 97) the Military Historical Society published an article by KD Pickup which included an image of an officer's helmet plate. Of the universal star type, it omits the Garter and instead has a circle inscribed 'Sixth West York'. In the centre of the circle, a rose. Mr Pickup notes that the item was silver plate in three parts and that the rose was on a black leather ground.

The 4th Yorkshire (West Riding) Rifle Volunteer Corps wore green home service helmets with star plates which had the arms and crest of Halifax—a man's head dripping with blood with a halo on a chequered

ground and the word 'Hales' above and 'Fax' below—within a strap inscribed '4th West York Rifle Volr Corps'. The corps was re-designated as the regiment's 1st Volunteer Battalion in 1883. Both officers' and other ranks helmet plates are illustrated in Dixon Pickup's book, *West York Rifle Volunteers 1859-1887*.

From Huddersfield, the 6th Yorkshire (West Riding) Rifle Volunteer Corps would be re-designated as 2nd Volunteer Battalion Duke of Wellington's Regiment in 1883. Dixon Pickup illustrates an other ranks white metal star plate which has a rose in the centre of a strap inscribed '6th West York R.V. Corps'. Mr Pickup also makes reference to an officer's blue cloth helmet being sold at an auction in April 1962, but gives no description.

Forming 'F', 'G', 'H' and 'J' Companies of the 6th Yorkshire (West Riding) Rifle Volunteer Corps in 1880 was the 34th (Saddleworth) Corps and an officer's helmet plate is illustrated in *West York Rifle Volunteer*. Of a star pattern, if has a stringed bugle in the centre of a strap inscribed, 'Saddleworth' at the bottom, and 'God And Fatherland' at the top.

Illustrations

103 An officers' Victorian helmet plate. (*Bruce Bassett-Powell and Bob Bennet*)

104 Richard Simkin's Supplement No 70, from his 'Military Types' series for the Army and Navy Gazette, showing two officers and a bugler who has his chinstrap hooked up behind the helmet.

105 Original artwork by J McNeill which includes an image of the Duke's crest and motto with his painting of a signaller. (*Anne SK Brown Military Collection, Brown University Library*)

Durham Light Infantry

Late 68th (Durham Light Infantry) and 106th Bombay Light Infantry Regiments

Dress Regulations, 1883, 1891, 1894, 1900

On Helmet Plates: In silver, on a black velvet ground, a bugle with strings. On the universal scroll, 'The Durham Light Infantry.'

Dress Regulations, 1904, 1911

On Helmet Plates: In silver, on a dark green velvet ground, a bugle with strings. On the universal scroll, 'The Durham Light Infantry.'

Kipling and King show an officer's helmet plate as described in Dress Regulations, but with the title scroll reading 'The Durham Lt Infy' and mention that the fuller title appeared on a 'latter version.' The also illustrate an all gilding metal other ranks centre which has 'Durham' on the circle and a bugle with strings.

Illustrations

106 Officer's helmet plate with 'The Durham Lt Infy' title scroll. *Bruce Bassett-Powell and Bob Bennet)*

107 Other ranks all gilding metal helmet plate centre.

108 In this original watercolour painting by Harry Payne, the artist shows a guard-changing scene. Green home service helmets with king's crown plates are being worn, the green collars having brass bugle badges. *Anne SK Brown Military Collection, Brown University Library)*

109 A sentry presents arms as the drum major leads the troops back to barracks in this original artwork by Ernst Ibbetson. The artist has shown the men wearing the green facings of the former 68th Regiment. Regulations in 1881 had directed that all non-royal English regiments should wear white (see illustration 5 below), the green, however, not making a reappearance, according to uniform historian WY Carman, until 1832. (*Anne SK Brown Military Collection, Brown University Library*)

110 Richard Simkin's Supplement No 95 from his 'Military Types' series of prints issued with the Army and Navy Gazette. Published on 2 November 1895, the image shows the regiment with white collars and cuffs. It had been the requirement of the 1881 reorganisations that all non-royal English regiments should have white facings.

111 An other ranks white metal helmet plate centre to the 1st Volunteer Battalion. The regiment's 1st Volunteer Battalion had been provided by the 1st Durham Rifle Volunteer Corps which had its headquarters Durham City. Re-designation was in 1887.

112 The 2nd Durham Rifle Volunteer Corps from Bishop Auckland wore green uniforms with scarlet facings and in 1881 provided the regiment's 2nd Volunteer Battalion. A green helmet is illustrated with Maltese Cross helmet plate. The wording around the central circle reads, '2nd Durham Rifle Volunteer Corps'.

113 1st Volunteer Battalion other ranks helmet.

114 1st Volunteer Battalion officer's helmet plate. (*Brian Lodge*)

East Lancashire Regiment

Late 30th (Cambridgeshire) and 59th (2nd Nottinghamshire) Regiments

Dress Regulations, 1883, 1891, 1894, 1900, 1904, 1911

On Helmet Plate: In silver, on a black velvet ground, the Sphinx over Egypt. On the universal scroll 'The East Lancashire Regiment.'

The Sphinx with 'Egypt' had been awarded to the 30th Regiment for its services during the campaign of 1801 and could be seen at the base of the officers' helmet plates prior to 1881. The regimental number was displayed in the centre on a black velvet ground. Other ranks helmet plate centres also had the Sphinx over 'Egypt' in white metal, the wording on the circle being 'East Lancashire'.

Illustrations

115 Officers' Victorian crown helmet plate. (*Bruce Bassett-Powell and Bob Bennet*)

116 Colour plate from Her Majesty's Army by Walter Richards showing a private in marching order. The artwork is by Frank Feller.

117 Supplement No 67 in Richard Simkin's 'Military Types' series

produced for the Army and Navy Gazette and published on 1 July 1893. A good view of the back of the helmet, the metal line of the officer's being clearly seen in the painting.

118 The regiment had two volunteer battalions, the 1st with headquarters in Blackburn, the 2nd at Burnley. Illustrated is an other ranks helmet plate centre to the 2nd.

East Surrey Regiment

Late 31st (Huntingdonshire) Regiment and 70th (The Surrey) Regiments

Dress Regulations, 1883, 1891, 1894

On Helmet Plate: In silver on a black velvet ground, an eight-pointed star; on the star, badge as for collar, but smaller. [On a bright cut-silver star, the arms of Guildford, in silver, on a shield in frosted gilt or gilding metal, with burnished edges, surmounted by a gilt or gilding metal Crown]. On the universal scroll, 'The East Surrey Regiment.'

Dress Regulations, 1900, 1904, 1911

On Helmet Plate: In silver on a black velvet ground, an eight-pointed star; on the star, badge as for collar [On a bright cut-silver star, the arms of Guildford, in silver, on a shield in frosted gilt or gilding metal, with burnished edges, surmounted by a gilt or gilding metal Crown], but without the crown. On the universal scroll, 'The East Surrey Regiment.'

The arms of Guildford were adopted as a badge by the regiment in 1881, and the star an old badge of the Surrey Militia. The several descriptions in Dress Regulations indicate that the word 'Regiment' appeared both in full, and in abbreviated form on the title scroll, the latter version coming into use sometime between 1900 and 1904. Kipling and King show the other ranks helmet plate centre, taking the trouble to describe the Guildford arms in more detail by mentioning the

lion in front of the castle and the woolpack on either side. The authors also include an additional example of the centre. Unlike the first design, which has a bow tied at the intersection of the sprigs of laurel at the base, the second variety has not.

Illustrations

119 The officers' Victorian crown helmet plate with 'Regt.' on the title scroll. (*Bruce Bassett-Powell and Bob Bennet*)

120 The other ranks helmet plate with bow at the intersection of the laurel springs.

121 Richard Simkin's Supplement No 68 in his 'Military Types' series for the Army and Navy Gazette. Published on 5 August 1893, the print features the East Surrey Regiment and shows a mounted officer wearing the blue home service helmet, while his men appear in the white, foreign service, version. The same plates were worn on both helmets.

East Yorkshire Regiment

Late 15th (York East Riding) Regiment

Dress Regulations, 1883, 1891, 1894, 1900, 1904

On Helmet Plates: In gilt metal on a ground of black enamel, a laurel wreath on an eight-pointed star. Within the wreath the White Rose, in silver. On the universal scroll, 'The East Yorkshire Regt.'

Dress Regulations, 1911

On Helmet Plates: In gilt or gilding metal, on a ground of black enamel, a laurel wreath on an eight-pointed star. Within the wreath the White Rose, in silver. On the universal scroll, 'The East Yorkshire Regiment.'

Major Parkyn points out that 'there are on record no less than four oval shoulder-belt plates, one having an eight-pointed star with, in its centre, a red cross within a Garter.' He also notes that although the White Rose of York was 'an old badge of the regiment' it did not appear on any belt plates of buttons until after 1881. Writers

Arthur L Kipling and Hugh L King note in Volume One of *Head-dress Badges of the British Army*, that the abbreviated 'Regt.' in the title scroll of officers' helmet plates was changed to read 'Regiment' in 1894. This would, however, conflict with the information provided by Dress Regulations for 1900, which still gives the abbreviated form of the word. For the other ranks helmet plate centres the authors give, 'One circlet: *East Yorkshire*. In the centre:

An eight-pointed star with the White Rose of York in the centre, the Rose encircled by a laurel-wreath. All in gilding-metal except the Rose which is in white-metal.'

Illustrations

122 An officers' queen's crown helmet plate the full title with silver title scroll inscribed 'The East Yorkshire Regiment'. (*Bruce Bassett-Powell and Bob Bennet*)

123 From artist Frank Feller, a colour print featuring an officer seemingly posing for the artist as three other ranks chat in the background. The image appeared in Walter Richards's Her Majesty's Army published by JS Virtue & Co during the 1890s.

124 The East Yorkshire Regiment had two Territorial Force battalions, the 4th and 5th (Cyclist), both of which had their headquarters in Hull. From Walter Richards's four-volume authorative work, His Majesty's Territorial Army, we see Richard Caton Woodville's painting of a colour-sergeant of the 4th Battalion. As a background, the artist has shown two officers in conversation and a bugler tending the colonel's mount.

125 A splendid example of an officer's Victorian crown helmet in its original tin seen on sale at the Hemswell Antique Centre. (*Hemswell Antique Centre*)

Essex Regiment

Late 44th (East Essex) and 56th (West Essex) Regiments

Dress Regulations, 1883, 1891, 1894, 1900, 1904, 1911

On Helmet Plates: An oak-leaf wreath is substituted for the universal wreath. In silver, on a black velvet ground, the Castle and Key, with the Sphinx over Egypt above, and a scroll below, inscribed Montis Insignia Calpe. On the universal scroll 'The Essex Regiment.'

The castle, key and motto had been conferred on the 56th Regiment for its services during the defence of Gibraltar, 1779 to 1783. The Sphinx superscribed 'Egypt' had come from the 44th, the oak wreath, according to Major HG Parkyn in his *(Military) Shoulder-Belt Plates and Buttons*, a device adopted in 1881. The Sphinx on a black velvet ground appeared on the pre-1881 44th officers' helmet plates. The helmet plate centres for other ranks had 'Essex' on the circle and displayed the castle, key, motto and Sphinx over 'Egypt'. Examples have been noted with both two and three towered castles, Kipling and King giving the change as 1896.

Thanks to a fine website ran by Michael Wood ('Essex Military Badges') we have a comprehensive record of the badges worn by the Essex Regiment. Most welcome is his section dealing with the several volunteer battalion, four in number having been formed by the 1st to 4th Essex Rifle Volunteer Corps.

Illustrations

126 A fine example of an officers' helmet with its Victorian crown plate. The special pattern oak wreath can be clearly

seen, along with the silver Sphinx, castle and motto. The chin strap has been secured to the gilt hook at the rear of the helmet. (*coldstreammilitaryantiques.com*)

127 In this original painting by Harry Payne we see a corporal of the regiment wearing a king's crown helmet plate. The regiment's Essex arms collar badges can be seen on the white collar, the artist showing his subject wearing both the Queen's and King's Medals for South Africa. (*Anne SK Brown Military Collection, Brown University Library*)

128 For his Supplement No 80, published on 4 August 1894 with the Army and Navy Gazette, artist Richard Simkin has shown a party from the Essex Regiment in marching order and wearing the white foreign service helmet. The plates as those for its home service equivalent.

129 Officer's king's crown helmet plate. (*Michael Wood*)

130 Other ranks Victorian crown helmet plate. (*Michael Wood*)

131 Other ranks king's crown helmet plate. (*Michael Wood*)

132 1st Volunteer Battalion first pattern Maltese Cross helmet plate, silvered for officers, blackened for other ranks. Note how the tablet below the Sphinx has been left blank. The battalion was originally known as the 1st Essex Rifle Volunteer Corps, wearing green uniforms with black facings, and had been re-designated as 1st Volunteer Battalion in 1883. Headquarters moved from Ilford to Brentwood in 1890. (*Brian Lodge*)

133 1st Volunteer Battalion, second pattern officers' helmet plate. (*Brian Lodge*)

134 1st Volunteer Battalion, second pattern other ranks helmet plate. (*Michael Wood*)

135 2nd Volunteer Battalion helmet plate. Originally the 2nd Essex Rifle Volunteer Corps with headquarters in Braintree, re-designation as in 1883. (*Michael Wood*)

136 First pattern Maltese Cross-type helmet plate to the 3rd Volunteer Battalion. This had been the 3rd Essex Rifle Volunteer Corps (re-designation was in 1883). (*Michael Wood*)

137 Officer's second pattern helmet plate, 3rd Volunteer Battalion. (*Michael Wood*)

138 Other ranks second pattern helmet plate, 3rd Volunteer Battalion with Victorian crown. (*Michael Wood*)

139 Other ranks helmet plate, 3rd Volunteer Battalion with king's crown. (*Michael Wood*)

140 4th Volunteer Battalion Maltese Cross helmet plate. This had been the 4th Essex Rifle Volunteer Corps, re-designation being in 1883. (*Michael Wood*)

141 4th Volunteer Battalion, star type helmet plate. (*Michael Wood*)

142 Officer's gilt helmet plate, 44th Regiment.

143 Other ranks helmet plate centre with three-towered castle. (*Brian Lodge*)

144 Other ranks helmet plate centre, 4th Volunteer Battalion. (*Brian Lodge*)

Gloucestershire Regiment

Late 28th (North Gloucestershire) and 61st (South Gloucestershire) Regiments

Dress Regulations, 1883, 1891, 1894

On Helmet Plates: In silver, on a black velvet ground, the Sphinx over Egypt. On the universal scroll, 'The Gloucestershire Regiment.' Badge for back of helmet—In dead gilt metal, the Sphinx over Egypt within a laurel wreath.

Dress Regulations, 1900, 1904, 1911

On Helmet Plates: In silver, on a black velvet ground, the Sphinx over Egypt. On the universal scroll, 'The Gloucestershire Regiment.' Badge for back of helmet—In dead gilt or gilding metal the Sphinx over Egypt within a laurel wreath.

Most famous is the regiment's 'Back Badge' which commemorates the 28th's gallantry during the Battle of Alexandria in 1801 when it fought back-to-back as the French came on from both the front and rear. From this came the tradition of wearing a Sphinx badge both at the front and back of the headdress and nicknames such as 'Brass before and brass behind', and the 'Fore and Afts'. The other ranks helmet plate centres also displayed the Sphinx, the circle being inscribed 'Gloucestershire'.

Always grateful to dedicated collectors who take the time and trouble to study their badges and write their findings up for the benefit of us all, in this case we must thank Gloucestershire expert, Daniel Brinson. His wonderful book *Military Insignia of Gloucestershire* was published in 2009 and features on the cover a photograph of a young drummer boy in conversation with his drum major. Both wear home service helmets, the rear view of the boy clearly showing the back badge. Full of detailed line drawings of insignia, of interest here are those for the pre-1881 officers' helmet plates. For the 28th Regiment, the numeral '28' sits below a Sphinx and the word 'Egypt', both in silver, upon a black velvet ground. Also of the universal crowned star, wreath and Garter type, that for the 61st has the number in gilt in the centre on a black leather ground, The Sphinx and Egypt this time being placed at the base of the plate and upon the buckle of the Garter.

The Royal South Gloucester Militia, which provided the regiment's 3rd Battalion in 1881, wore green helmets. Daniel Brinson illustrates two officers' helmet plates which he dates '1878-1881'. Both are of the universal crowned star and wreath design with the Royal Crest as centre pieces on black velvet grounds. On the first plate the Royal Crest appears in the centre of the Garter and has a title scroll reading, 'Royal South Gloucester'. The second, however, carries the name, 'Royal South Gloucester Militia', this time on a circle which has replaced the Garter. The Royal North Gloucester Militia formed the 4th Battalion in 1881 and a helmet plate is described by Daniel Brinson as being of the usual star type with title scroll reading 'Royal North Gloucester Militia'. In silver plate, the item and the cypher 'VR' are on a black velvet ground.

Moving now to the Gloucestershire Rifle Volunteers. The 1st Corps from Bristol had a Maltese Cross plate displaying crossed rifles above the City of Bristol Arms and the motto 'In Danger Ready' in the centre of a circle inscribed '1 Glos City of Bristol R.V.'. Examples of this exist with both queen's and king's crowns. Daniel Brinson in his notes to this badge records that 'The Regimental committee did not approve the change from shako to helmet until January 1892 and Hobsons of London were given the contract.' He goes on to say that 'The change was completed by the end of the following year.' The plates were worn on the battalion's dark green helmets with a lighter green felt backing behind.

The 2nd Gloucestershire Rifle Volunteers also had Maltese Cross helmet plates, the centres having a stringed bugle in the centre of a circle inscribed '2nd Gloucestershire Rifle Volunteer Corps'. An example is illustrated by Daniel Brinson who notes that the officers' version was in blackened white metal with high points silvered and burnished. For other ranks, the plates were in blackened brass.

Under General Order 63 of May 1883, the 1st and 2nd Gloucestershire RVC were re-designated as 1st and 2nd Volunteer Battalions of the Gloucestershire Regiment. Referring to Daniel Brinson's book, we learn that the Bristol corps took on universal type star plates much like those of the Regulars. The author illustrates an officer's pattern which he describes as being in silver plate, the gilt Sphinx and 'Egypt' being

Illustrations

145 The jacket of Military Insignia of Gloucestershire by Daniel Brinson.

146 The officers' post-1881 gilt and silver helmet plate as described in Dress Regulations. (*Bruce Bassett-Powell and Bob Bennet*)

147 The other ranks gilding metal plate.

148 A good view of the back badge in an original watercolour painting by Harry Payne, in which we see an officer returning the salute of a sentry.

149 From the brushes of Ernest Ibbetson, a group of bandsmen painted for one of his Gale & Polden postcards.

150 Back view of helmet showing position of the back badge. (*Bob Bennet*)

151 Maltese Cross-type helmet plate to the 1st Gloucestershire Rifle Volunteer Corps.

on a black velvet ground. An additional scroll displayed the title '1st Volunteer Battalion'. From Gloucester, the 2nd Volunteer Battalion retained their Maltese Cross-type helmet plates, the circle, however, now reading, '2nd Volr. Batt Gloucestershire'. The officers' plates were in white metal, those for other ranks in blackened brass.

A 3rd Volunteer Battalion had been raised at Bristol in 1900 which wore a slouch hat decorated with very dark green cockerel's feathers. In 1908, the now three volunteer battalions transferred to the Territorial Force as the regiment's 4th, 5th and 6th Battalions. The battalions now required new helmet plates and subsequently the 4th and 6th Battalions, which had adopted scarlet tunics with white facings, took on the same patterns as were then in use by the Regulars. The tablets below the Sphinx, however, were required to be left blank. The 5th was to retain its rifle style dress and with it the busby.

Long associated with the Gloucestershire Rifle Volunteers was the cadet corps formed at Cheltenham College. The company was attached to the 2nd Volunteer Battalion until becoming a contingent with the Junior Division Officer Training Corps in 1909, save for an affiliation to the 1st Gloucestershire Volunteer Engineers between 1889-1903. Daniel Brinson illustrates two helmet plates: a universal crowned star and wreath in blackened brass and with a bugle in the centre of a circle inscribed, 'Cheltenham College Rifles'. The second plate is from the Royal Engineers period and comprised the Royal Arms with scrolls inscribed '1st Glou. V.E' and 'Cheltenham College Cadets'.

Gordon Highlanders

Late 75th (Stirlingshire) and 92nd (Gordon Highlanders) Regiments

WY Carman, in his book on Richard Simkin, records that the 75th Regiment wore standard infantry dress up until 1881 and includes a watercolour by the artist which shows an officer and private wearing blue home service helmets.

There were, between 1881 and 1908, seven volunteer battalions, the records of which were included in Lieutenant-General Sir James Moncrieff Grierson's *Records of the Scottish Volunteer Force 1859-1908*. On 8 December 1879, the 1st Aberdeenshire Rifle Volunteer Corps was given authority to change their uniform to scarlet doublets with yellow facings, Gordon tartan trews and blue helmets. General Order 12 of 1

Illustrations

152 General Grierson's colour plate of a colour-sergeant of the 1st Aberdeenshire Rifle Volunteer Corps in 1880.

153 6th Volunteer Battalion. General Grierson's painting of a captain wearing a grey uniform with black facings and belts, the officer standing next to a sergeant wearing the glengarry and scarlet doublet introduced in January 1891.

February 1884 notified the re-designation of the corps to 1st Volunteer Battalion Gordon Highlanders and with this came another change in dress. This time to that of the Gordons, less the feather bonnet which was replaced by the glengarry. The 2nd Aberdeenshire Rifle Volunteer Corps, which would provide the 2nd Volunteer Battalion in 1884, wore blue helmets for a short time between 1878 and 1880. The 6th Volunteer Battalion in 1887 adopted grey helmets with silver ornaments.

Governors of Military Prisons

Dress Regulations, 1883, 1891
Helmet: Blue cloth, with gilt plate representing the Royal Arms.

Dress Regulations, 1900
Helmet: Blue cloth. Gilt or gilding metal plate—the Royal Arms.

Dress Regulations, 1904
Helmet: Blue cloth. Helmet plate—the Royal Arms.

Hampshire Regiment

Late 37th (North Hampshire) and 67th (South Hampshire) Regiments

Dress Regulations, 1883, 1891, 1894, 1900, 1904, 1911
On Helmet Plate: On a black velvet ground, the Royal Tiger, in gilt metal, within a laurel wreath, in silver. On the universal scroll 'The Hampshire Regt.'

The 67th regiment's Royal Tiger badge was authorized on 20 December 1826 in recognition of its services in India 1805-26 and it appeared on the pre-1881 home service helmet on a black velvet ground together with the number '67'. The Tiger was also used on the other ranks all gilding metal helmet plate, the wording on the circle being 'Hampshire'.

Illustrations

154 The post-1881 officers' Victorian crown helmet plate. (*Bruce Bassett-Powell and Bob Bennet*)

155 In Richard Simkin's 'Military Types' Supplement No 73 for the Army and Navy Gazette, two officers chat as members of the regiment take a break from a field exercise. The image was published on 6 January 1894.

156 Other ranks white metal helmet plate, 2nd Volunteer Battalion. With headquarters in Southampton, this was the former 2nd Hampshire Rifle Volunteer Corps.

157 Other ranks white metal helmet plate, 3rd Volunteer Battalion. With headquarters in Portsmouth, this was the former 3rd Hampshire Rifle Volunteer Corps.

158 Other ranks helmet plate, 2nd Hampshire Rifle Volunteer Corps, the rose being from the arms of Southampton, the headquarters of the battalion. This corps was re-designated as 2nd Volunteer Battalion in 1885.

Herefordshire Regiment

Star plates were worn by both officers and other ranks of the 1st Hereford Rifle Volunteer Corps, the central device being the shield, with its three lions, from the City of Hereford arms. The corps served as a volunteer battalion (without change in title) of the King's (Shropshire Light Infantry) from 1881 until becoming the Herefordshire Regiment (Territorial Force) in 1908. At this time, both the officers' and other ranks star helmet plates displayed the City of Hereford arms within the Garter, but this time complete with supporters of two lions.

Hertfordshire Regiment

When the Territorial Force was created in 1908 the idea was proposed that the 1st and 2nd Volunteer Battalions of the Bedfordshire Regiment should take on the title of 6th (Hertfordshire) Battalion Bedfordshire Regiment. This proposal was, however rejected, and for several months former volunteers appeared in official records as 'The Hertfordshire Battalion' Bedfordshire Regiment. The battalion was soon, however, re-designated as the Hertfordshire Regiment and as such was independent of Bedfordshire. JD Sainsbury, in his book *Hertfordshire's Soldiers,* shows a photograph of three officers in 1909, all wearing home service helmets. Kipling and King illustrate an officer's star helmet plate which has a hart lodged in the centre on a black velvet ground within a strap inscribed 'The Hertfordshire Regiment'. There exists, what must be a scarce item: a helmet plate with the title scroll reading 'Hertfordshire Battalion'.

Illustration

159 Officer's helmet plate with 'The Hertfordshire Battalion' title scroll.

Highland Light Infantry

The Regular battalions of the Highland Light Infantry did not wear the home service helmet. Several of the regiment's volunteer battalions did, however, and images of these appeared in *Records of the Scottish Volunteer Force 1859-1908* by Lieutenant-General Sir James Moncrieff Grierson.

Illustrations

160 In 1880, the 6th Lanarkshire Rifle Volunteer Corps (later to become the 2nd Volunteer Battalion) replaced their shakos with blue helmets with silver ornaments. These were worn until 1906 when blue Balmoral bonnets became the battalion's sole headdress. From Records of the Scottish Volunteer Force 1859-1908 by Lieutenant-General Sir James Moncrieff Grierson, images of a corporal and field officer wearing blue helmets.

161 Blue helmets were issued to the 31st Lanarkshire Rifles in 1878. Two years later the corps was re-designated as 8th (The Blythswood) Rifle Volunteers then by General Order 181 of 1 December 1887, as the 3rd Volunteer Battalion Highland Light Infantry. The uniform of the regiment, complete with its shako, had been adopted the year before. In

General Grierson's colour plate, which also includes the uniforms of the 5th Lanarkshire Rifle Volunteer Corps (last three figures), we see a private for the period 1878-86 wearing the helmet.

162 In 1880 the 9th Lanarkshire Rifle Volunteer Corps replaced their shakos with blue helmets. In the following year, the 9th became a volunteer battalion of the Highland Light Infantry, but no change in title took place. The helmet was retained until 1904 when HLI shakos were taken into use. Here, in illustration (3) we see another of General Grierson's colour plates, this time showing a private wearing the scarlet doublet with yellow facings, and Mackenzie tartan trews authorised for wear in 1883.

163 An officer's helmet, 6th Lanarkshire Rifle Volunteer Corps. (*Benny Bough*)

164 An officer's helmet with white metal and gilt plate. (*Benny Bough*)

Inspector of Military Prisons

The Royal Arms.

King's (Liverpool Regiment)

Late 8th (The King's) Regiment

Dress Regulations, 1883, 1891, 1894, 1900, 1904

On Helmet Plates: In silver, on a crimson velvet ground, the White Horse, with scroll above inscribed in old

English capitals, Nec aspera terrent. On the universal scroll 'The Liverpool Regiment.'

Dress Regulations, 1911

On Helmet Plates: In silver, on a crimson velvet ground, the White Horse, with scroll above inscribed in old English capitals, Nec aspera terrent. On the universal scroll 'The Liverpool Regiment.' Above the Garter a silver scroll inscribed 'The King's.'

The White Horse and motto *Nec aspera terrent* (Difficulties do not daunt) had been directed to be worn within the Garter on appointments in 1716. The officers' helmet plate in use prior to 1881 displayed the White Horse of Hanover in silver and standing on a gilt ground. Below this were the Roman numerals 'VIII' in gilt, the whole set upon a red velvet ground. An illustration of this item can be seen on page 111 of *Headdress Badges of the British Army* (Volume One) by Arthur L Kipling and Hugh King.

Turning now to the Volunteers and Territorials associated with the regiment, I am indebted to a useful series of articles that appeared in the *Bulletin of the Military Historical Society* from November 1953 written by John H Brown. The 1st Lancashire Rifle Volunteer Corps, which would become the regiment's 1st Volunteer Battalion and later, 5th Territorial Battalion, had a Maltese Cross-type helmet plate with a stringed bugle horn and the numeral 'I' in the centre of a circle inscribed 'Lancashire Rifle Volunteers.' Having been re-designated as 1st Volunteer Battalion by Army Order 81 of March 1888, the helmet plates remained much the same except that the circle was now inscribed 'Vol. Bn. King's Liverpool.' For the 5th Battalion, John H Brown gives the following: 'All white metal Maltese cross surmounted by King's Crown. In the centre a cross stringed bugle, the whole surrounded by laurel wreath, below a scroll inscribed "5th Bn. The King's Liverpool Regiment."'

The 5th Lancashire Rifle Volunteer Corps would take on the designation of 2nd Volunteer Battalion in 1888, the helmet plate prior to that being a white metal Maltese Cross, the centre of which had a 'Liver Bird' (from the city arms) on a red ground and within a circle inscribed 'Liverpool Rifle Volunteer Bde.' Above the circle, and below the crown, there was a scroll inscribed 'Fifth', another being placed below the cross inscribed 'Lancashire.'

The regiment's 6th Volunteer Battalion was provided by the former 19th Lancashire Rifle Volunteers, a corps raised at the beginning of 1861 from men employed in the newspaper and printing trades. John H Brown provides the following: '…all white metal helmet plate of the same format as the Regular Battalion, with the additional scroll, "6 V.B."'

Illustrations

165 The first post-1881 plate, as described in the 1900 Dress Regulations. In 1911 and additional scroll inscribed 'The King's' was placed between the top of the Garter and the crown. (*Bruce Bassett-Powell and Bob Bennet*)

166 An other ranks helmet, the White Horse in white metal is shown in the centres minus the Nec aspera terrent scroll. (*Stuart Bates*)

167 The original artwork provided by artist Edgar Holloway for one of Gale and Polden's postcard sets featuring a sergeant and two privates during guard changing. (*Anne SK Brown Military Collection, Brown University Library*)

168 A white metal star plate similar in design to that of the Regulars was worn by the officers of both the 3rd and 4th Volunteer Battalions who wore scarlet jackets with blue facings. That for the 4th VB is illustrated and it can be seen that the White Horse and title scrolls, unusually, are in gilt.

169 Other ranks all white metal plate for the 4th Volunteer Battalion.

170 The 1st Isle of Man Rifle Volunteer Corps was re-designated as 7th (Isle of Man) Volunteer Battalion King's (Liverpool Regiment) under Army Order 81 of March 1888. Illustrated is the other ranks white metal helmet plate with its three legs in armour, flexed at the knee, symbol of the Isle of Man.

King's Own Malta Regiment of Militia

Dress Regulations, 1891, 1894

Helmet Plate: A Maltese Cross in gilt metal, surmounted by the Crown. On the Cross, a scroll in silver, inscribed 'Royal Malta Militia, MDCCC.'

Dress Regulations, 1900, 1904, 1911

Helmet Plate: A Maltese Cross in gilt or gilding metal, surmounted by the Crown. On the Cross, a scroll in silver, inscribed 'Royal Malta Militia, MDCCC.'

The battle honour '1800' was granted in recognition of the services of the Malta Militia during the siege of 1798-1800, the title 'King's Own' being awarded after a visit to the island by King Edward VII in in 1903.

Illustration

171 Helmet plate as described in Dress Regulations.

King's Own (Royal Lancaster Regiment)

Late 4th (The King's Own) Regiment

Dress Regulations, 1883, 1891, 1894

On Helmet Plates: In silver, on a scarlet velvet ground, the Lion of England. On the universal scroll 'Royal Lancaster Regt.'

Dress Regulations, 1900, 1904

On Helmet Plates: In silver, on a crimson velvet ground, the Lion of England. On the universal scroll 'Royal Lancaster Regt.'

Dress Regulations, 1911

On Helmet Plates: In silver, on a crimson velvet ground, the Lion of England. On the universal scroll 'Royal Lancaster Regiment.' Above the Garter, a silver scroll inscribed 'The King's Own.'

The Lion of England on its own, above or below a crown, is the ancient badge of the regiment. It was given by William III as a reward for its services after his 1688 landing in England. A most comprehensive history of the regiment was written by Colonel L I Cowper in 1939 which provides extensive detail on uniform and badges. Regarding the Lion badge, he notes that it first appeared on the shoulder-belt plates in 1774 and it was then shown without a crown and with the paw raised as in the Royal Standard. In 1822 the paw was depicted lowered and hovering close to the ground. It appears raised again in 1855.

Kipling and King describe the pre-1881 officers' helmet plate as: 'On a black-velvet ground the Lion of England above the Roman numerals *IV*. The laurel-wreath in gilt for the 1st Battalion and silver for the 2nd Battalion.' The Lion also appeared on the other ranks helmet plate centres, the circles reading 'Royal Lancaster'.

In August 1971, the Military Historical Society (*The Bulletin* No 85) published a superbly researched article by member David A Rutter. Titled 'The Volunteer Movement in Ulverston, Lancashire, 1803-1967', the item shows two star pattern helmet plates to the 1st Volunteer Battalion King's Own (Royal Lancaster Regiment). Both, one and officer's, the second an other ranks pattern, have Victorian crowns and Lion centres. The circle of the latter has the wording '1st Volr. Batt. Royal Lancaster', both items being dated by Mr Rutter as 'c1883-1902'.

Illustrations

172 The first officers' post-1881 helmet plate: In silver, on a scarlet velvet ground, the Lion of England. On the universal scroll Royal Lancaster Regt. (*Bruce Bassett-Powell and Bob Bennet*)

173 In 1900, the ground in the centre of the officers' helmet plates was changed to crimson and, in 1911, the title on the universal scroll was altered to The Royal Lancaster Regiment. A new additional scroll was also placed above the Garter inscribed The King's Own. This is the plate illustrated. (*Bruce Bassett-Powell and Bob Bennet*)

174 The other ranks Victoria crown helmet plate. In brass, it displays the Lion in the centre and title, 'Royal Lancaster', on the circle.

175 In full regalia, his decorations including the Victoria Cross won as a young officer during the Indian Rebellion of 1857, we see in illustration (4) a photograph of Field Marshal Frederick Sleigh Roberts inspecting a guard of honour provided by the King's Own. We can date the image as post-1902 as the helmet plates clearly show a King's crown. Roberts died after contracting pneumonia while visiting Indian troops at St Omer, France on 14 November 1914.

176 Harry Payne's detailed watercolour featuring a sergeant in conversation with another soldier as two bandsmen chat in the background. Visible is a lion helmet plate centre, the medals (Queen's and King's for South Africa) suggesting a date of post-Second Boer War. (*Anne SK Brown Military Collection, Brown University Library*)

177 A painting by Richard Simkin showing the helmet being worn by a private of the regiment as others stand around in service dress. (*Anne SK Brown Military Collection, Brown University Library*)

178 An other ranks, white metal helmet plate for the 1st Volunteer Battalion. The plate has a separate centre secured to the backplate via two split pins, one passing through two lugs arranged north and south, the other from east to west. Formerly the 10th Lancashire Rifle Volunteer Corps, the 1st VB had its headquarters at Ulverston.

King's Own Scottish Borderers

Late 25th (The King's Own Borderers) Regiment

Dress Regulations, 1883

On Helmet Plates: In silver, on a black velvet ground, the Castle of Edinburgh. On the universal scroll 'The King's Own Borderers'.

Dress Regulations, 1891, 1894, 1900

On Helmet Plates: In silver, a thistle wreath; within the wreath a circle pierced with the designation 'King's Own Scottish Borderers.' Above the circle a scroll surmounted by the Royal Crest. The scroll pierced with the motto In veritate religionis confide. Over the circle, the Cross of St Andrew in burnished silver. On the cross, the Castle of Edinburgh. On the wreath at the bottom of the circle, a scroll with the motto in relief, Nisi Dominus frustra.

Dress Regulations, 1904

On Helmet Plates: Not worn. Note: The helmet had been replaced by the Kilmarnock bonnet that year.

Along with the 'King's Own' title in 1805 came the regiment's Royal Crest badge and the motto *In veritate religious confide* (I put my trust in the truth of religion). Featured also on the badges, and authorized 8 March 1832, is the Castle of Edinburgh together with the city's motto *Nisi Dominus frustra* (Without the Lord everything is in vain). The White Horse of Hanover had been displayed on the Colours previous to 1805, the Sphinx superscribed 'Egypt', authorized in 1802, commemorating the campaign of the previous year.

The first post-1881 officers' helmet plate displayed Edinburgh Castle in silver on a black velvet ground, the title then being 'The King's Own Borderers.' The title of the regiment was changed in 1887 to 'King's Own Scottish Borderers', as seen in illustration (179). From 1881 to 1884 the other ranks helmet plate centre was the usual round type. Edinburgh Castle featured in the centre, the circle having 'King's Own Borderers.' From 1884, until the change of title in 1887, a white metal badge similar in design to that worn on the helmets of officers was placed on the star plate.

179

Illustrations

179 Officer's gilt and silver helmet plate.

180 Bassoon player, the image from Bands of the British Army by WJ Gordon. Artwork by Frederick Stansell. Helmets were not worn after 1904.

181 The regiment's 2nd Volunteer Battalion was formed by the 1st Berwickshire Rifle Volunteer Corps, the illustration being an officer's silver helmet plate.

181

180

182

182 Forming the 3rd Volunteer Battalion was the 1st Dumfriesshire Rifle Volunteer Corps which assumed the uniform of the regiment in 1888, the helmet not being worn after 1900.

183 Two pre-1881 officers, artist Richard Simkin who dates his watercolour '1878' being quick to record the regiment in its new home service helmet. (*Anne SK Brown Military Collection, Brown University Library*)

King's Own (Yorkshire Light Infantry)

Late 51st (2nd Yorkshire, West Riding) or King's Own Light Infantry and 105th (Madras Light Infantry) Regiments

Dress Regulations, 1883,
  On Helmet Plates: In silver, on a black enamel ground, a French horn with the White Rose in the centre; on the scroll below, Cede Nullis. On the universal scroll, 'The South Yorkshire Regiment.'

Dress Regulations, 1891, 1894, 1900, 1904, 1911
  On Helmet Plates: In silver, on a black enamel ground, a French horn with the White Rose in the centre. On the universal scroll, 'The King's Own Yorkshire Light Infantry.'

The White Rose of York was an old badge of the 51st Regiment. A French bugle-horn, rather than the usual type was, according to tradition, adopted after Waterloo where the 51st had defeated a French regiment of mounted chasseurs whose badge it was. *Cede Nullis* was the motto of the 105th Regiment. The change in title scroll, as indicated in Dress Regulations for 1891 was in recognition of the regiment's title changing from The King's Own Light Infantry (South Yorkshire Regiment) to The King's Own Yorkshire Light Infantry in 1887.

A French horn in silver, together with the numerals 51 in the curl, and a silver rose above the Garter, featured on the star plates of the 51st Regiment's officers' helmet plates. Post-1881 examples have been noted with title scrolls reflecting both titles. There were two patterns of other ranks helmet plate centres, both being illustrated by Kipling and King whose descriptions I use: (1) 'On a circlet: *South Yorkshire*. In centre: A bugle with strings. Within the strings, the Rose of York and, below the bugle, a scroll inscribed *Cede Nullis*. All in gilding-metal. Worn from 1881 to 1887.' (2) 'On circlet: *The Yorkshire Light Infantry*. In centre: A French horn with the White Rose of York in the curl. The Rose in white-metal, remainder in gilding-metal.' The second centre, because of the length of the new title, does not have the usual laurel spray at the bottom.

Military Historical Society editor Gary Gibbs wrote an interesting article in 2003 (*The Bulletin,* No 213) entitled, 'Defence Not Defiance' in which he showed images of four helmet plates to the 1st Volunteer Battalion. The 5th Yorkshire (West Riding) Rifle Volunteer Corps had become part of the King's Own Light Infantry (South Yorkshire Regiment) in 1881, changing its designation to 1st Volunteer Battalion under General Order 14 of February 1883. Two of the plates are shown here in illustrations 8 and 9. The other two are queen's crown officers' examples of the Regular's plates, one with the 'South Yorkshire' title scroll, the other with the later wording.

Illustrations

184 Officers' helmet plate with original 'South Yorkshire Regiment' title scroll. (*Bruce Bassett-Powell and Bob Bennet*)

185 Officers helmet plate with the post-1887 title scroll and revised centre excluding the Cede Nullis motto. (*Bruce Bassett-Powell and Bob Bennet*)

186 Officers' helmet plate with king's crown.

187 The regiment's Minden Day tradition of wearing roses in the helmets, Aldershot, 1 August 1909. Queen's crown helmet plates are being worn.

188 A Harry Payne postcard featuring a corporal and private wearing king's crown helmet plates and French horn collar badges.

189 Richard Simkin's Supplement No 87 from his 'Military Types' series for the Army and Navy Gazette. The colour plate was published on 2 March 1895.

190 An officer's silvered helmet plate suggesting a possible militia item. The regiment's 3rd Battalion had been provided by the 1st West York Militia.

191 An officer's-style helmet to the 1st Volunteer Battalion with a 'South Yorkshire' title and curved tablet just below the crown inscribed 'Defence Not Defiance', that often used motto of the 1859-1908 Volunteer Movement. (Gary Gibbs)

192 An other ranks version of illustration No 8 above. (Garry Gibbs)

King's Royal Rifle Corps
Late 60th King's Royal Rifle Corps

Dress Regulations, 1883

On Helmet Plates: In bronze, a Maltese cross with scroll, at the top, inscribed Celer et Audax. Above the top scroll, the crown. On the Cross a circle inscribed 'The King's Royal Rifle Corps', within the circle, on a scarlet cloth ground, a bugle with strings. A Lion between each division of the cross; and on each division, the battles of the Regiment. The dimensions are – from the top of the Cross to the bottom of the plate, back measurement, 3 6/8 inches; extreme width 2½ inches.

Dress Regulations, 1891

On Helmet Plates: In bronze, a Maltese cross surmounted by the Royal Crown resting *on a tablet, inscribed Celer et Audax. On the Cross a circle inscribed 'The King's Royal Rifle Corps', within the circle, a bugle with strings on a scarlet cloth ground. On each division of the cross, the battles of the Regiment. The dimensions are – from the top of the Cross to the bottom of the plate, back measurement, 4 inches; extreme width 2½ inches. Note: The busby had replaced the helmet the year before.*

The Regiment's volunteer battalions were provided by several rifle volunteer corps from Middlesex and London.

Illustrations

193 Helmets were worn from 1878 and until 1890 when the busby was reintroduced. The helmet plate is illustrate, this example with '60' in the strings of the bugle. (Bruce Bassett-Powel and *Bob Bennet*) , *Stuart Bates* (2)

194 Officer's helmet. Note the absence of '60' within the strings of the bugle. (*Stuart Bates*)

195 From Richard' Simkin's Our Armies, this plate shows an officer and several riflemen.

196 Artist, PW Reynold's fine study of a mounted officer. This colour plate being published with the 1913 Appendix volume to The Annals of the King's Royal Rifle Corps for which SM Milne supplied the uniform notes. Regarding the helmet he wrote, 'In 1878 the busby was superseded by a helmet made of black felt with bronze binding, spike, chain, and plate.' He goes on to say that the helmet plate was a large cross, 'adopted for all ranks with a crown of proportionate size; the points were without knobs, but the lions between the limbs were retained; the scrolls were smaller, and the centre of the circle was perforated, showing the bugle and '60' in relief over scarlet cloth.'

197 Sketch of the helmet plate from The Annals of the King's Royal Rifle Corps which mentions that in 1881 the number 60, 'was eliminated from all clothing, badges, and buttons.'

198 The 3rd London Rifle Volunteer Corps. This corps, seen here waring home service helmets with ball fittings, served as a volunteer battalion (without change in title) until transferring to the Territorial Force in 1908 as the 3rd London Regiment.

199 Lance-Corporal, 3rd London Rifle Volunteer Corps.

King's (Shropshire Light Infantry)

Late 53rd (Shropshire) and 85th (The King's Light Infantry) Regiments

Dress Regulations, 1883, 1891, 1894

On Helmet Plates: In silver, on a ground of dark green velvet, a bugle with strings. In gilt metal within the strings of the bugle, the monogram K.L.I. On the universal scroll, 'King's Shropshire Lt. Infty.'

Dress Regulations, 1900

On Helmet Plates: In silver, on a frosted gilt or gilding metal centre, a bugle with strings. In gilt or gilding metal within the strings of the bugle, the cypher K.L.I. On the circle, 'Shropshire Light Infantry.'

Dress Regulations, 1904, 1911

On Helmet Plates: In silver, on a ground of dark green enamel, a bugle with strings. In gilt or gilding metal within the strings of the bugle, the cypher K.L.I. On the universal scroll, 'King's Shropshire Lt. Infty.'

The original 1881 title had been The King's Light Infantry (Shropshire Regiment), the change to The King's (Shropshire Light Infantry) coming in the following year. For the pre-1881 officers' helmet plates, Kipling and

King record two types: (1) 'The numerals *53* in the centre. Below the Garter a scroll inscribed *The Shropshire Regiment.*' (2) 'As above, but without the scroll.' Also mentioned is the 85th Regiment's plate which had '85' within the strings of a bugle. The other ranks helmet plate centres had a bugle with 'Shropshire' on the circle.

The 1st Shropshire Rifle Volunteer Corps, which became 1st Volunteer Battalion King's (Shropshire Light Infantry) in 1887, wore star pattern helmet plates which featured as its central device the three loggerheads (leopards' faces) from the county arms. Historian G Archer Parfitt illustrated several items belonging to the Shropshire Rifle Volunteers in the August 1967 edition of the *Bulletin of the Military Historical Society,* among them two star plates (officers' and other ranks) for the 1st Volunteer Battalion. Both have bugle horns in the centre. He also shows two Maltese Cross-type plates (officers' and other ranks again) with bugle centre pieces. These he attributes to the 2nd Shropshire Rifle Volunteer Corps for the period 1880-1908.

Illustrations

200 The 1st Battalion King's Light Infantry in 1881 were stationed at Chatham and it would seem that although home service helmets were then in use, star plates had yet to be fitted. In this photograph of the band, clearly seen in use are the plates from the pre-1878 shakos.

201 The last pattern shako plate as seen being worn on the home service helmets of the 1st Battalion Band in 1881 (see illustration 1).

202 Sketch of the 85th Regiment's officers' helmet plate from *The 85th King's Light Infantry* which was published by Spottiswoode & Co in 1913 and edited by CRB Barrett.

203 Officer's Victorian crown helmet plate. (*Bruce Bassett-Powell and Bob Bennet*)

204 Original watercolour painting by Harry Payne featuring a sergeant and corporal wearing king's crown helmet plates. (*Anne SK Brown Military Collection, Brown University Library*)

205 Colour plate from *The 85th King's Light Infantry* regimental history showing (second from right) a sergeant wearing the home service helmet.

206 Painting by the late Bob Marrion showing an officer and private of the 2nd Shropshire Rifle Volunteer Corps which was re-designated as 2nd Volunteer Battalion King's Shropshire Light Infantry in 1887.

Lancashire Fusiliers

Late 20th (East Devonshire) Regiment

The use of the home service helmet by the 20th Regiment would have been for a short period only before it took on Fusilier distinctions in 1881. Kipling and King illustrate an officer's star helmet plate which they describe as: 'On a black-velvet ground the numerals *20* in gilt. Below the Garter the Sphinx superscribed *Egypt.*' This honour commemorates the services of the 20th during the campaign of 1801.

Illustrations

207 From Volume II of A History of the Lancashire Fusiliers by Major B Smyth, a private in 1880.

208 An original watercolour by Richard Simkin featuring two officers. (Anne SK Brown 1military Collection, Brown University Library)

Leicestershire Regiment

Late 17th (Leicestershire) Regiment

Dress Regulations, 1883, 1891, 1894, 1900. 1904, 1911

On Helmet Plates: On a black velvet ground, the Royal Tiger in silver, with silver scroll above, inscribed 'Hindoostan.' On the universal scroll, 'Leicestershire Regiment.'

To commemorate the services of the 17th Regiment in India during the period 1804 to 1823, HM King George IV conferred the badge of the Royal Tiger superscribed 'Hindoostan' on 25 June 1825. The officers' pre-1881 helmet plates showed this device above the numeral '17' all in silver. Examples of the post-1881 officers' plates have been noted with both 'Leicestershire Regiment' and 'The Leicestershire Regiment' title scrolls. Lieutenant-Colonel EAH Webb's history of the 17th Regiment mentions that 'The' was placed before 'Leicestershire Regiment' sometime between 1900 and 1904. Other ranks helmet plate centres had 'Leicestershire' on the circles and the Royal Tiger with 'Hindoostan' in the center.

The Leicestershire Militia wore a helmet plate, described by Kipling and King as follows: 'An eight-pointed star, the topmost point displaced by a Victorian crown. On this a laurel-wreath and within this a circlet inscribed *Leicestershire Militia* and in the centre the Irish Harp. On the base of the wreath a scroll inscribed *Vestigia nulla retrorsum*. In gilt for officers.'

Illustrations

209 A cigarette card from John Player, showing an officer's pre-1881 helmet.

Note how the metal strip that runs down from the top of the helmet terminates a few inches inside of the back peak. Lieutenant-Colonel EAH Webb, in his history of the 17th Regiment, mentions that the helmet was not taken into use until 1879.

210 The officers' pre-1881 helmet plate as illustrated in Lieutenant-Colonel EAH Webb's history of the 17th Regiment.

211 Officer's Victorian crown helmet plate with silver Royal Tiger and 'Hindoostan' in the centre and 'The Leicestershire Regiment' silver title scroll. (*Bruce Bassett-Powell and Bob Bennett*)

212 The other ranks, all gilding metal, helmet plate centre.

213 Richard Simkin's Supplement No 56 for his Army and Navy Gazette 'Types' series was published on 6 August 1892 and shows several other ranks in firing positions, with an officer looking on.

Lincolnshire Regiment

Late 10th (North Lincoln) Regiment

Dress Regulations, 1883, 1891, 1894, 1900, 1904, 1911

On Helmet Plates: In silver, on a black velvet ground, the Sphinx over Egypt. On the universal scroll 'The Lincolnshire Regt.'

The regiment had served in the 1801 Egyptian campaign, for which they were authorised to wear the badge and honour of a Sphinx superscribed 'Egypt'. The pre-1881 officers' helmet plates had the Sphinx over 'Egypt' with below, the numeral '10'. After becoming the Lincolnshire Regiment, the battle honour was again used for both the officers' and other ranks helmet plate centres. In Volume One of *Head-dress Badges of the British Army,* the authors show an officer's plate with the wording of the title scroll as recorded in Dress Regulations. Noted, however, is a later plate which has the spelling 'Regiment' in full.

In 1881 the Royal South Lincolnshire Militia provided the regiment's 3rd Battalion. Kipling and King illustrate an officer's helmet plate with the following description: 'An eight-pointed star, the topmost point displaced by a Victorian crown. On this a laurel-wreath. Within the wreath a circlet inscribed *South Lincolnshire Regiment.* In the centre a lion's head on a wreathed scroll. Dark-blue ground to centre. In silver-plate.'

Illustrations

214 Officers' helmet plate with 'Regiment' in full silver title scroll. (*Bruce Bassett-Powell and Bob Bennet*)

215 Both officers' and other ranks helmet plates are being worn in this image by Richard Simkin published on 6 February 1892 as a supplement to the Army and Navy Gazette. Note how the artist has been careful to indicate the metal edging to the front peaks of the officers' helmets.

216 Regulations demanded that Territorial battalions could not display any battle honours awarded to their parent regiment. A Sphinx device was permitted, however, but this could not be shown together with the word 'Egypt'. The Lincolnshire Regiment had two Territorial Force battalions, the 4th with headquarters in Lincoln and the 5th which was located in Grimsby. Illustrated is an officer's helmet plate for the post-1908 period with the tablet below the Sphinx left blank.

217 Officers' white metal helmet plate to the 2nd Volunteer Battalion at Grantham.

London Regiment

The London Regiment was a Territorial Force regiment created in 1908. Comprising twenty-six battalions, the numbering in fact went up to twenty eight, the twenty-sixth and twenty-seventh positions being left vacant. Besides those mentioned below, the following helmet plates are mentioned by Kipling and King. In October 1912, the original 10th Battalion at Paddington was disbanded, and its place taken by a new 10th in Hackney. Kipling and King illustrate an officers plate with the following description: 'An eight-pointed star, the topmost point displaced by an Imperial crown. On this a laurel-wreath and within this the Garter with, in the centre within a laurel-wreath, an eight-pointed star, the topmost point displaced by a crown. On the star a circlet inscribed *Justitia turris nostra* and within this a tower on ground from the Seal of the Borough of Hackney. Below the Garter a three-part scroll inscribed *Tenth London Hackney*. The device in the centre and the title-scroll in silver-plate, remainder in gilt with black-velvet backing to the centre.'

For the 15th Battalion, the Prince of Wales's Own Civil Service Rifles, Kipling and King illustrate an officer's helmet plate with the following description: 'An eight-pointed star, the topmost point displaced by an Imperial crown. On this a laurel-wreath and within this the Garter with, in the centre, the Prince of Wales's plumes, coronet and motto. All gilt except the Prince of Wales's plumes and motto. A black-velvet background to the centre.'

For officers of the 24th (The Queen's) Battalion, Kipling and King

give: 'An eight-pointed star, the topmost point displaced by an Imperial crown. On this a laurel-wreath and within this the Garter. In the centre the Paschal Lamb. Below the Garter a scroll inscribed *24th Battn. The London Regiment*. The centre and title-scroll in silver plate, remainder in gilt. A red-velvet backing is worn in the centre.' The other ranks gilding metal plate had the Lamb within a circle inscribed, '24 County (T) of London – The Queen's'.

Illustrations

218 7th (City of London) Battalion London Regiment, other ranks helmet plate. Formed by the former 3rd London Rifle Volunteer Corps, the description given by Kipling and King is as follows: 'A star of eight points, the topmost point displaced by an Imperial crown. On this an oak-wreath with crossed Mace and Sword of State superimposed. Within the wreath a circlet inscribed Domine dirign nos with the numeral 7 in the centre. Across the base of the wreath a scroll inscribed City of London and below this a shield bearing the Arms of the City of London. In gilding-metal.' The mace, sword and motto are also from the city arms. Kipling and King also describe the officers' plate: 'A star of eight points, the topmost point displaced by an Imperial crown. On this an oak-wreath with crossed Mace and Sword of State superimposed. Within the wreath a circlet inscribed Domine dirign nos with in the centre. A fused grenade with the numeral 7 on the ball. Across the base of the wreath a scroll inscribed City of London and below this a shield bearing the Arms of the City of London. In gilt except for the numeral 7, on the ball of the grenade, which is in silver-plate.' (*Brian Lodge*)

219 13th (County of London) Battalion The London Regiment (Kensington) with 'South Africa 1900-1902' battle honour just visible either side of the shield. The central device is the arms of the London Borough of Kensington. Kipling and King refer to this plate as an other ranks item. (*Brian Lodge*)

220 13th (County of London) Battalion London Regiment (Kensington). Kipling and King refer to this as an officers' item and show the same plate, but with the addition of a scroll at the bottom inscribed, 'South Africa 1900-02'. (*Brian Lodge*)

221 19th (County of London) Battalion London Regiment. The white metal centre is the arms of the London Borough of St Pancras. This is the officers' version, Kipling and King illustrating a gilding metal plate without the South Africa honour for other ranks. (*Brian Lodge*)

222 Officer, 7th (City of London) Battalion, painted in 1989 by Brian Fosten.

Loyal North Lancashire Regiment

Late 47th (The Lancashire) and 81st (Loyal Lincoln Volunteers) Regiments

Dress Regulations, 1883, 1891, 1894, 1900, 1904, 1911

On Helmet Plates: In silver, on a black velvet ground, the Royal Crest. Below the Crest, the Rose of Lancaster in gilt metal and red and green enamel. On the universal scroll, 'Loyal North Lancashire Regiment.'

The Royal Crest, which was also that of the Duchy of Lancaster, was an old badge of the 47th Regiment, as was the Red Rose of Lancaster. The other ranks helmet plate centres were in gilding metal with the Royal Crest and Rose. The circles had the title, 'Loyal North Lancashire'.

Illustrations

223 The officers' gilt, silver and red and green enamels helmet plate with Victorian crown. (*Bruce Bassett-Powel and Bob Bennett*)

224 An original watercolour painting by Harry Payne. Both men are wearing the home service helmet, the collar badges being the arms of the city of Lincoln, an old badge of the 81st Regiment.

225 An other ranks white metal helmet plate centre used in conjunction with a crown to form a glengarry badge.

226 Much the same design as the Regular officers' helmet plate, this specimen for the 2nd Volunteer Battalion is all in white metal save for the Rose which is in the usual gilt and red and green enamel.

227 A corporal bugler of the 2nd Volunteer Battalion, his helmet with a Victorian crown plate, just visible at his side.

Manchester Regiment

Late 63rd (West Suffolk) and 96th Regiments

Dress Regulations, 1883, 1891, 1894, 1900, 1904, 1911

> On Helmet Plates: In silver, on a black velvet ground, the Arms with motto of the City of Manchester. On the universal scroll, 'The Manchester Regiment.'

The arms of the City of Manchester were adopted as a badge with the title in 1881. The 96th had the Sphinx superscribed 'Egypt' and this appeared in the centre of the pre-1881 officers' helmet plates. The other ranks helmet plate centres had the Manchester arms with 'Manchester' on the circle. In David A Rutter's article on the fleur de lis badge worn by the Manchester Regiment (Military Historical Society, *The Bulletin*, No 80, May 1970), an officer's star plate to the 4th Volunteer Battalion is illustrated. Unusual in design, it omits the Garter, the centre having a fleur de lis. The author adds a note stating that there is reason to doubt that this plate was ever worn, as '…the Battalion wore Helmet plates of the usual design with the city arms in the centre.'

David Rutter also contributed to the Military Historical Society in November 1974 (*The Bulletin* No 98), this time with an article on the Manchester Rifle Volunteers. Photographs of two helmet plates are included with the article: an officer's star pattern with Victorian crown and the City arms in the centre, and an other ranks version which also has the Manchester arms. The circle is inscribed 'Manchester' at the top, and 2nd Volr Battn' at the bottom.

Illustrations

228 Officer's Victorian crown helmet plate. (*Bruce Bassett-Powell and Bob Bennet*)

229 An original watercolour painting by Harry Payne. (*Anne SK Brown Military Collection, Brown University Library*)

230 Gale & Polden postcard, 'Changing the Guard', by Ernest Ibbetson.

231 Gale and Polden postcard, 'Commanding Officer, Adjutant and Sergeant Major', by Ernest Ibbetson.

232 Richard Simkin's Supplement No 92 of his 'Military Types' series, published with the Army and Navy Gazette on 3 August 1895.

233 Colour plate after Richard Caton Woodville published with His Majesty's Territorial Army by Walter Richards.

Military Foot Police

Formed in 1885, the Military Foot Police merged with the Military Mounted Police as the Corps of Military Police in February 1926. An informative article on the badges and buttons of the Royal Military Police appeared in the May 1972 edition of *The Bulletin of the Military Historical Society*. By Lieutenant-Colonel NW Poulsom, the item explained that upon the formation of the MFP, 'there would appear to have been no distinctive Military Police cap badge.' He goes on to say that a universal helmet plate with the cypher 'VR' was the only badge in use. Colonel Poulsom illustrates two helmet plates, a Queen's crown version, and another which has a king's crown and the cypher 'ERVII'. Kipling and King point out that the letters in the centre had a red cloth backing. Interestingly, they also illustrate an Edward VII helmet plate with a queen's crown.

Illustration

234 Ernest Ibbetson's original artwork for one of Gale & Polden's postcard sets showings the helmet being worn. *Anne SK Brown Military Collection, Brown University Library*

Military Mounted Police

Formed in 1877, the Military Mounted Police merged with the Military Foot Police as the Corps of Military Police in February 1926. An informative article on the badges and buttons of the military police appeared in the May 1972 edition of *The Bulletin of the Military Historical Society*. By Lieutenant-Colonel NW Poulsom, the item explained that upon the formation of the MMP, 'there would appear to have been no distinctive Military Police cap badge.' He goes on to say that a universal helmet plate with the cypher 'VR' was the only badge in use. Colonel Poulsom illustrates two helmet plates, a Queen's crown version, and another which has a king's crown and the cypher 'ERVII'. Kipling and King point out that the letters in the centre had a red cloth backing. Interestingly, they also illustrate an Edward VII helmet plate with a queen's crown. Except for the quartermaster, who wore a cocked hat, there were no officers in the MMP.

Illustration

235 Ernest Ibbetson's original 1909 artwork for one of Gale & Polden's postcard sets shows the helmet being worn. The other soldier wearing the cap badge introduced in 1904. (*Anne SK Brown Military Collection, Brown University Library*)

Military Provost Staff Corps

The Royal Arms.

Norfolk Regiment

Late 9th (East Norfolk) Regiment

Dress Regulations, 1883, 1891, 1894, 1900, 1904, 1911

On Helmet Plates: The figure of Britannia, in silver, on a black velvet ground. On the universal scroll 'The Norfolk Regiment.'

Several accounts regarding the use of the figure of Britannia by the 9th Regiment of Foot exist. In 1948 reference to the distinction was made by General Bainbridge upon the occasion of the regiment receiving new Colours, 'This distinguishing badge', he remarked, 'was given to you for your gallantry at the battle of Almanza.' That battle took place in 1707, but Loraine Petre, in his history of the regiment, refers to a letter dated 9 March 1797 which states that the Britannia design had been awarded three years later after the fighting at Saragossa. No authority for its use, however, appeared in the Royal Warrants of 1747, 1751 or 1768. Certainly, the distinction had found its way to the Colours by 1802. There is also a Horse Guards letter dated 3 March 1800 stating that HM the King had granted permission for the badge 'some time ago.' It was, in fact, confirmed as the regiment's ancient badge in 1799. Seeing Britannia during the Peninsular War, a Spanish soldier, thinking it was the Virgin Mary, knelt and crossed himself. This was the origins of the regiment's 'Holy Boys' nickname.

Kipling and King in Volume 1 of their *Head-dress Badges of the British Army* show a Victorian crown officer' helmet plate which follows the 1900 Dress Regulations description (page 123, item 222). The photograph shows Britannia's hand resting on her knee, the authors then going on to say that a later version had the hand raised. Other ranks plates also exist with hands in both positions, the circles always with 'Norfolk'. The centres are recorded in *Head-dress Badges* as being in gilding metal with Britannia in white metal.

Headquarters of the 3rd Norfolk Rifle Volunteer Corps (later 3rd Volunteer Battalion) were at East Derham and a selection of diary records from the vicar there, the Rev Benjamin Armstrong, were published by the Military Historical Society in November 1991 (*Bulletin* No 166). Of interest here is the following, '8th September 1878. In afternoon I preached to the local Company of Volunteers, who appeared in their new scarlet uniform and black helmets – an immense improvement on the old grey uniforms.'

Illustrations

236 Officers' helmet plate, the latter version with Britannia's hand raised. (Bruce Bassett-Powell, and Bob Bennet)

237 An original watercolour by Harry Payne who shows a sergeant wearing both the Queen's and King's Medals for South Africa. The second man wears the crossed flags of a signaller. (Anne SK Brown Military Collection, Brown University Library)

238 An other ranks helmet plate centre, Britannia with her hand raised.

239 An other ranks helmet plate with an all-white metal as Britannia on a red ground.

Northamptonshire Regiment

Late 48th (Northamptonshire) and 58th (Rutlandshire) Regiments

Dress Regulations, 1883, 1891, 1894, 1900, 1904, 1911

On Helmet Plates: In silver, on a black velvet ground, the Castle and Key; on a scroll above, 'Gibraltar,' on a scroll below, 'Talavera.' On the universal scroll 'The Northamptonshire Regiment.'

The Gibraltar Castle, key and motto (*Montis insignia Calpe,* The badge of the Rock of Gibraltar) were authorized as a badge on 2 May 1836, the 58th having served during the defence of the Rock between 1779-83. The battle honour 'Talavera' was awarded to the 48th.

The pre-1881 officers' helmet plate for the 48th Regiment is illustrated by Kipling and King (item 195) with the following description: 'On a black-velvet ground the numerals *48* in gilt.' The Gibraltar Castle on the first post-1881 officers' helmet plates was originally shown with two towers. In 1900, however, and in accordance with a War Office instruction dated 30 January, the castle was redesigned with three. Kipling and King shows an example of the early version. The other ranks plates were also subject to the same change in castle design. 'Gibraltar' on a scroll above the castle, and another below with 'Talavera', were included in both, as was the circle title of 'Northamptonshire'.

Part of the Army reorganisations of 1881 saw the Northampton and Rutland Militia re-designated as the 3rd Battalion Northamptonshire Militia. The battalion officers wore a fine star-type helmet plate, an example of which was illustrated in the May 2001 (No 204) edition of the *Bulletin of the Military Historical Society*. The Cross of St George appears in the centre of the Garter which has a scroll above inscribed 'Northamptonshire', and one below with '& Rutland Militia'. Below the lower scroll is a horseshoe, that symbol long associated with Rutland. Sprigs of oak are placed between the scrolls.

Illustrations

240 For the other ranks helmet plate of the 1878-1881 period we turn the Bulletin of the Military Historical Society (No 200, May 2000) and an article by member John Denton on the badges of the Northamptonshire Regiment. Clearly photographed is a universal star plate with '48' within the Garter. (*John Denton*)

241 An officers' helmet plate, the castle having three towers. (*Bruce Bassett-Powell and Bob Bennet*)

242 Richard Simkin's Supplement No 83, published as part of his 'Military Types' series for the Army and Navy Gazette on 3 November 1894.

243 Officer's helmet with Maltese Cross plate. The regiment's only volunteer battalion had its headquarters in Northampton and wore grey uniforms with scarlet facings.

Northumberland Fusiliers

Late 5th (Northumberland) (Fusiliers) Regiment

The helmet was not worn by the Regular battalions.

Illustrations

244 The 1st Volunteer Battalion had grey helmets with Maltese Cross plates, the centre of which displayed the figure of St George and the Dragon. The title of the battalion was placed on the circle and reads, '1st Vol Bat Northumberland Fusiliers', and the regimental motto, Quo fata vocant, appears on the lower arm of the cross.

245 From an old cigarette card, a private of the 1st Volunteer Battalion on 'Sentry Go' wearing an all grey uniform with red collar, cuffs and piping.

246 From the 1st Volunteer Battalion, an officer's grey helmet with a Victorian crown star plate. The 1st VB had its headquarters at Hexham. (*Stuart Bates*)

Ordnance Store Corps / Army Ordnance Corps

The Ordnance Store Corps was formed in 1881 and re-named as Army Ordnance Corps on 20 June 1896.

Dress Regulations, 1883, 1891, 1894
    Helmet: As for Infantry; plate with O.S.C. in centre, on a black ground.

Dress Regulations, 1900, 1904, 1911

On the Helmet: The Ordnance Arms in silver, on a black velvet ground.

Writing in May 1980 (*Bulletin of the Military Historical Society,* No 120), Charles Thomas notes for other ranks a 'standard brass crown-and-star plate, with inserted bar bearing a script 'OSC' monogram, all in brass or g/m. In the same article, the author illustrates the scarce first other ranks post-June 1896 helmet plate, a universal star plate with the letters ''AOC' in the centre of the Garter. Plates with the Ordnance arms in white metal were later used.

Illustrations

247 A fine officer's gilt plate with silver 'OSC' on black velvet. Writing in May 1880 (Bulletin of the Military Historical Society, No 120), Charles Thomas dates this plate as 1881 to 1896. For the corresponding other ranks plate, he records: 'standard brass crown-and-star plate, with inserted bar bearing a script 'OSC' monogram, all in brass or g/m.' (*Bruce Bassett-Powell and Bob Bennet*)

248 Army Ordnance Corps officer's Victorian crown helmet plate. (*Bruce Bassett-Powell and Bob Bennet*)

249 Army Ordnance Corps officer's helmet with king's crown plate. (*Stuart Bates*)

Oxfordshire and Buckinghamshire Light Infantry

Late 43rd (Monmouthshire Light Infantry) and 52nd (Oxfordshire Light Infantry) Regiments

Dress Regulations, 1883, 1891, 1894

On Helmet Plates: In silver, on a ground of black enamel, a bugle with strings. On the universal scroll 'The Oxfordshire Lt. Infy.' The plate is of gilding, not gilt metal.

Dress Regulations, 1900, 1904

On Helmet Plates: In silver, on a ground of black enamel, a bugle with strings. On the universal scroll 'The Oxfordshire Lt. Infy.'

Dress Regulations, 1911

On Helmet Plates: In silver, on a ground of black enamel, a bugle with strings. On the universal scroll 'The Oxfordshire and Buckinghamshire Lt. Infy.'

'Buckinghamshire' had been added to the title of the regiment in 1908. The first other ranks helmet plate

centre was in gilding metal with a bugle in the centre and 'Oxfordshire' on the circle. After 1908 the wording was changed to 'Oxfordshire & Buckinghamshire'.

The 1st Buckinghamshire Rifle Volunteer Corps wore grey uniforms with scarlet facings, the helmets being of the Maltese Cross type with lions between the arms. An example can be seen in the Military Historical Society's 'Badge Notes' for February 2016 *(The Bulletin,* No 263). The centre circle has the title, 1st Bucks Rifle Volunteer Corps and within this, the chained swan from the arms of Buckingham.

Illustrations

250 This Queen's crown gilt officers' plate has a silver bugle horn on a black ground as described in Dress Regulations prior to 1911. As can be seen, the silver title scroll carries the title The Oxfordshire Lt. Infy. *(Bruce Bassett-Powell and Bob Bennet)*

251 A post-1901 officer's helmet with king's crown and the original, 'The Oxfordshire Lt. Infy.' title scroll. It may just be through dirt, but both the bugle horn and title scroll seem not to be the required silver. The chin strap has been secured to the hook on the back of the helmet and clearly visible are the ventilation holes at the base of the spike.

252 An other ranks post-1908 helmet plate in gilding metal with king's crown, as would be expected for this date, and the circle now reflecting the new title assumed in 1908.

253 This colour print is Richard Simkin's Supplement No 79 in his 'Military Types' series produced for the Army and Navy Gazette. Published on 7 July 1894, the scene shows an officer observing a firing party while another from a distance judges the men's musketry expertise through binoculars.

254 As both civilians and soldiers watch, the 2nd Battalion Oxfordshire and Buckinghamshire Light Infantry are seen here just having arrived at Aldershot Station in 1911. The Colours are cased and unusually the men are wearing their full dress home service helmets with khaki service dress. This mixed dress was often seen during the 1911 railway strike, the helmet offering, albeit limited, protection from rioters. Memorable is the riot that took place at Llanelli in which six people died during clashes between railway workers and troops.

255 Other ranks helmet plate to the 1st Oxfordshire (Oxford University) Rifle Volunteer Corps. This corps was re-designated the 1st (Oxford University) Volunteer Battalion by General Order 181 of December 1887. The central device of the white metal plate is the open book and three crowns that feature in the university coat of arms.

256 Other ranks helmet plate, 2nd Oxfordshire Rifle Volunteer Corps. With headquarters in Oxford, this corps was re-designated as 2nd Volunteer Battalion by General Order 181 of December 1887. The device in the centre of the helmet plate is an ox crossing a ford, the play on words charge from the city arms.

257 Other ranks helmet, 2nd Buckinghamshire Rifle Volunteer Corps. With headquarters at Eton College, members of the 2nd Buckinghamshire (Eton College) RVC wore grey uniforms with light blue facings. It was designated as 4th (Eton College) Volunteer Battalion in 1887, but reverted to its former title in 1902. The grey helmet in the illustration has a special white metal badge consisting of a small bugle over the intertwined letters, EVRC. (*Stuart Bates*)

258 Although this photograph would have been taken after the creation of the 4th Battalion in 1908, the two officers are still wearing Victorian crown helmet plates. Just visible on the King's Colour is the Roman numeral IV.

Prince Albert's (Somersetshire Light Infantry)

Late 13th (1st Somersetshire) (Prince Albert's Regiment of Light Infantry)

Dress Regulations, 1883, 1891, 1894, 1900, 1904, 1911

On Helmet Plates: In silver, on a black velvet ground, a bugle with strings, surmounted by a mural crown with scroll above inscribed 'Jellalabad'; the Sphinx over Egypt within the strings of the bugle. On the scroll, 'Somersetshire Light Infantry.'

The badges of the 13th were the Sphinx superscribed 'Egypt', which was authorized in July 1802 to commemorate the services of the regiment in the campaign of the previous year, and the Mural Crown

which was given with the battle honour Jellalabad in 1842. A light infantry bugle-horn came with the title in 1822, and the cypher of Prince Albert twenty years after that.

Two pre-1881 officers' helmet plates are recorded in Volume One of *Head-dress Badges of the British Army* as follows*:* '(1) On a black-velvet ground a bugle-horn surmounted by a mural crown and above this a scroll inscribed *Jellalabad*. Within the strings of the bugle the Roman numerals '*XIII*'. All in silver. (2) As above but with the numerals '*13*' in gilt.'

As can be seen from the information provided by Dress Regulations, the title scroll on the officers' helmet plate read 'Somersetshire Light Infantry'. The Army List would suggest that the shortening of the county name would have occurred sometime around 1912, but certainly there are officers' helmet plate with Victorian crowns that have 'Somerset'. The other ranks, all brass, helmet plate centres also displayed the mural crown, Sphinx and bugle, the circle having 'Somersetshire'.

Illustrations

259 An other ranks pre-1881 universal crowned star helmet plate. The number is detachable.
260 Officers' helmet plate with 'Somerset Light Infantry' silver title scroll. (*Bruce Bassett-Powell and Bob Bennet*)
261 Other ranks helmet plate centre.
262 A fine photograph of an officer taken in the Taunton studio of photographer H Montague Cooper. He wears the home service helmet, his collar badges being of gold and silver embroidery, the buttons having a bugle in the centre of a circle inscribed 'The Prince Alberts'. The same designation appears around the circle of the waist-belt clasp, the silver ornament as for the helmet plate centre.
263 By Richard Simkin, this colour plate was produced as a supplement to the Army and Navy Gazette and published on 4 July 1891. Signed and dated 1891, the image features from left to right, a bugler, colour-sergeant and an officer.
264 Both the County School at Wellington and King's College in Taunton provided cadet corps affiliated to the 2nd Volunteer Battalion Somersetshire Light Infantry. Here in illustration (264) we see a young cadet wearing a grey uniform with black piping, the helmet having a Maltese Cross plate.

Prince of Wales's Leinster Regiment (Royal Canadians)
Late 100th (Prince of Wales's Royal Canadian) and 109th (Bombay Infantry) Regiments

Dress Regulations, 1883

On Helmet Plates: In silver, on a black velvet ground, the Prince of Wales's Plume over two maple leaves. On a scroll, beneath the leaves, 'Central India.' On the universal scroll, 'Prince of Wales's Leinster Regiment.'

Dress Regulations, 1891, 1894, 1900, 1904

On Helmet Plates: In silver, on a black velvet ground, the Prince of Wales's Plume over two maple leaves. On a scroll, beneath the leaves, 'Central India.' On the universal scroll, 'Prince of Wales's Leinster Regiment.' The Coronet in gilt or gilding metal.

Dress Regulations, 1911

On Helmet Plates: In silver, on a black velvet ground, the Prince of Wales's Plume over two maple leaves. The Coronet in gilt or gilding metal. On a scroll, beneath the leaves, 'Central India.' On the universal scroll, 'Prince of Wales's Leinster Regiment.'

The Prince of Wales's badge and maple leaves had come from the 100th Regiment, 'Central India' from the 109th. Other ranks helmet plate centres also had the Prince of Wales's insignia, crossed maple leaves and a scroll inscribed 'Central India'. The plumes and motto in white metal, remainder in gilt.

Illustrations

265 Published on 1 August 1896, Richard Simkin's Supplement No 104 in his 'Types of the British Army' series shows a tall wall, the top of which is covered in what could be barbed wire or some similar material designed to defeat unwanted visitors. Outside a private wearing one good conduct stripe has just stepped forward from his sentry box which, although a snug fit for a Victorian soldier of average build, would offer some protection from rain and wind. He stands to attention and is pleased to see the party of men marching in single file towards him. They have come to relieve him. Blue home service helmets are being worn so we can assume that Simkin has looked to the 1st Battalion for inspiration who, in 1896, were stationed in Ireland. The facings are blue, the helmet plate centres displaying the plumes, coronet and motto of the Prince of Wales whose name had been associated with the regiment since 1858.

266 An other ranks helmet plate centre. Also seen on the device are two crossed maple-leaves, recalling the Canadian connection, and a scroll inscribed 'Central India'. Just 'Leinster' from the title appears on the circle.

267 An officer's helmet plate with a Victorian crown. (*Bruce Bassett-Powell and Bob Bennet*)

268 An officer's helmet with king's crown.

Prince of Wales's (North Staffordshire Regiment)

Late 64th (2nd Staffordshire) and 98th (The Prince of Wales's) Regiments

Dress Regulations, 1883, 1891, 1894, 1900, 1904, 1911

On Helmet Plates: In silver, on a black velvet ground, the Prince of Wales's Plume. On the universal scroll, 'The North Staffordshire Regiment.'

The 98th had been linked with the Prince of Wales in 1876, the plumes, coronet and motto appearing on a red velvet ground appearing two years later on the new helmets. In 1881 the other ranks helmet plate centres also displayed the Prince of Wales's device, the wording on the circle reading 'North Staffordshire'. The regiment had two volunteer battalions and a photograph of an other ranks helmet plate to the 2nd Volunteer Battalion was included in an article written by PG Smith and published by the Military Historical Society in February 1981 (*The Bulletin,* No 123). In white metal, the plate has the Prince of Wales's plumes, coronet and motto in the centre and '2nd Volr Battn North Staffordshire' on the circle. Mr Smith's photograph also shows the helmet plate centre being used in conjunction with a Victorian crown as a glengarry badge.

Illustrations

269 Officer's helmet plate with Victorian crown. (*Bruce Bassett-Powell and Bob Bennet*)

270 Officer's helmet with king's crown. (*Stuart Bates*)

271 A fine original watercolour painting of a mounted officer by Richard Simkin.

272 In this image by Richard Simkin three members of the regiment seem to have found their way into a walled garden. A corporal is seen peering over a wall, his ladder steadied by a private, while grateful for a lull in the proceedings, another with his helmet off squats in a handy wheelbarrow. Part

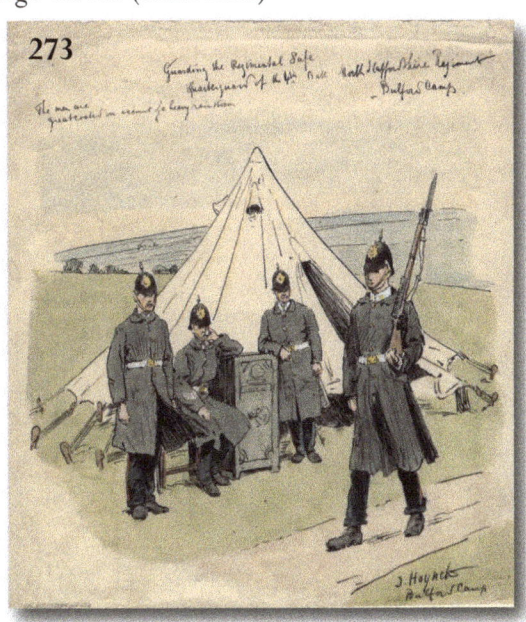

of Simkin's 'Military Types' series, the plate was published with the Army and Navy Gazette on 7 September 1895.

273 By Jan Hoynk van Papenrecht (1858-1833) this delightful watercolour shows the unusual scene of four members of the 4th Battalion North Staffordshire Regiment at Bulford Camp in 1899, 'guarding the Regimental safe'. (*Anne SK Brown Military Collection, Brown University Library*)

Prince of Wales's Own (West Yorkshire Regiment)

Late 14th (Buckinghamshire) or The Prince of Wales's Own) Regiment

Dress Regulations, 1883, 1891, 1894, 1900

On Helmet Plates: In silver, on a black velvet ground, the White Horse, with motto Nec aspera terrent on a scroll above. On the universal scroll, 'The West Yorkshire Regiment.'

Dress Regulations, 1904

On Helmet Plates: In silver, on a red velvet ground, the White Horse, with motto Nec aspera terrent on a scroll above. On the universal scroll, 'The West Yorkshire Regiment.'

Dress Regulations, 1911

On Helmet Plates: In silver, on a scarlet velvet ground, the White Horse, with motto Nec aspera terrent on a scroll above. On the universal scroll, 'The West Yorkshire Regiment.'

The White Horse and motto *Nec aspera terrent* (Difficulties do not daunt) was authorized to be displayed on the Queen's Colour in February 1873. The White Horse and motto were to form the centre, together with the numeral '14', of the pre-1881 officers' helmet plates. Other ranks helmet plate centres displayed the White Horse in white metal without the motto, the brass circle being inscribed 'West Yorkshire'.

Illustrations

274 The badge, as described in Dress Regulations. In Volume One of Head-dress Badges of the British Army, the authors note: 'In 1904, the ground in the centre was changed to red-velvet and, in 1911, to scarlet-velvet.' (*Bruce Bassett-Powell and Bob Bennet*)

275 Ernest Ibbetson's original artwork for one of Gale & Polden's postcard series.

The ranks present arms and the King's Colour is lowered to the ground as members of the Royal Family are about to pass. (*Anne SK Brown Military Collection, Brown University Library*)

276 Headquarters of the regiment's 2nd Volunteer Battalion were in Bradford. White metal star plates were worn, the illustration showing how the helmet plate centre was used in conjunction with a crown to form the glengarry badge.

Prince of Wales's Volunteers (South Lancashire Regiment)

Late 40th (2nd Somersetshire) and 82nd (Prince of Wales's Volunteers) Regiments

Dress Regulations, 1883, 1891, 1894, 1900, 1904, 1911

On Helmet Plates: In silver, on a black velvet ground, the Sphinx over Egypt. On the universal scroll 'South Lancashire Regiment.'

The Sphinx and 'Egypt' honour had been awarded to the 40th Regiment for its services during the campaign of 1801. Pre-1881 officers' helmet plates have been noted for both the 40th and 82nd Regiments. The 40th had its gilt number in the centre on a black velvet base, a Sphinx superscribed 'Egypt' appearing in silver just below the Garter. The 80th displayed no badge, its number being displayed on a black velvet ground in the centre. The other ranks post-1881 helmet plate centres displayed the Sphinx above 'Egypt' in white metal, the circle title being 'South Lancashire'.

Illustrations

277 Officer's helmet plate with Victorian crown. (Illustration credit: *Bruce Bassett-Powell and Bob Bennet*)

278 Richard Simkin's Supplement No 76 from his 'Military Types' series for the Army and Navy Gazette, published on 7 April 1894.

279 A silvered metal officer's helmet plate to the 2nd Volunteer Battalion.

Princess Charlotte of Wales's (Royal Berkshire Regiment)

Late 49th (or the Princess Charlotte of Wales's or Hertfordshire) and 66th (Berkshire) Regiments

Dress Regulations, 1883, 1891, 1894, 1900, 1904, 1911

On Helmet Plates: In silver, on a scarlet cloth ground, a Stag under an oak. On the universal scroll 'The Berkshire Regiment.'

The device of a stag under an oak tree, associated with the County of Berkshire for centuries, was an old badge in use by the Royal Berkshire Militia and taken into use by the regiment in 1881. Other ranks helmet

plate centres also displayed the stag under an oak, the circles initially being inscribed with 'Berkshire', then after 1885, 'Royal Berkshire'. Major HG Parkyn in his article on English Militia regiments (*Journal of the Society for Army Historical Research,* Vol 15, 1936) noted that the Stag and oak tree were taken into use as a badge on the helmets in 1881 by all battalions of the regiment. Besides the 3rd Battalion, formally the Royal Berkshire Militia, there was a 1st Volunteer Battalion which had its headquarters in Reading.

Illustrations

280 Officers' helmet plate with black silver stag and oak tree on a black ground and 'The Berkshire Regiment' silver title scroll. (*Bruce Bassett-Powel and Bob Bennet*)

281 The officers' post-1886 helmet plate, now with scarlet cloth backing and 'Royal Berkshire Regiment' title scroll. (*Bruce Bassett-Powel and Bob Bennet*)

282 An original watercolour painting by Harry Payne showing a detailed side view of a private from the regiment. Note his Dragon of China collar badge, an honour awarded to the 49th Regiment for services during the China War of 12840-1842. *Anne SK Brown Military Collection, Brown University Library*)

283 Richard Simkin's Supplement No 84 in his 'Military Types' series for the Army and Navy Gazette. Published on 1 December 1884, the image shows, in addition to the home service helmet, glengarry and forage caps being worn.

284 The 3rd Battalion band at Pernham Camp in 1913. Dragon of China collar badges are being worn, the helmet plates still with queen's crowns.

285 Other ranks king's crown helmet plate. Visible through the centre is the split pin that secured the separate centre to the back of the plate. (emedals)

286 With a scarlet cloth backing and 'Royal Berkshire' title, an other ranks helmet plate to the 1st Volunteer Battalion. (*coldstreammilitaryantiques.com*)

287 An other ranks helmet plate centre used with the addition of a crown as a glengarry badge. Usually separate items held in place via a brass backplate and split pins inside the cap, some specimens do exist as one-piece items.

Princess Louise's (Argyll and Sutherland Highlanders)

Late 91st (Princess Louise's Argyllshire) Highlanders and 93rd Regiments

The home service helmet was not worn by the regular battalions of the regiment. The regiment from 1881 to 1908 had seven volunteer battalions however, details of which were recorded by Lieutenant-General Sir James Moncrieff Grierson in his book *Records of the Scottish Volunteer Force 1859-1908*. He recalls that in 1881 the 1st Renfrewshire Rifle Volunteer Corps adopted grey helmets with

Illustrations

288 The various uniforms worn by the 1st and 2nd Volunteer Battalions and their predecessors as illustrated by Lieutenant-General Sir James Moncrieff Grierson in his book Records of the Scottish Volunteer Fore 1859-1908.

289 The various uniforms worn by the Dumbartonshire Rifle Volunteers. Clearly visible is the Maltese Cross helmet plate worn by the lieutenant second from the right in the picture. The plate, with its four lions between the arms of the cross, is of a universal type and displays in the centre of a circle inscribed 'Dumbartonshire Rifle Volunteers', the elephant from the arms of Dumbarton. Illustration from Lieutenant-General Sir James Moncrieff Grierson's Records of the Scottish Volunteer Fore 1859-1908.

bronze ornaments. The corps became the 1st (Renfrewshire) Volunteer Battalion by General Order 181 of 1 December 1887 and on 13 December 1889 was given sanction to assume the uniform of the regiment, its headdress then being the glengarry.

The 2nd Renfrewshire Rifle Volunteer Corps changed their grey for scarlet tunics in 1875, adding to this the blue helmet as a replacement for the shako in 1881. Having been re-designated as 2nd (Renfrewshire) Volunteer Battalion in 1887, the uniform of the Argyll and Sutherland Highlands was assumed in April 1898. Helmets were retained until 1903.

Although serving as the regiment's 6th volunteer battalion, the 1st Dumbartonshire Rifle Volunteer Corps did not assume the title in 1887. Helmets with bronze ornaments were introduced on 17 November 1881, the uniform at the time being green with scarlet facings. On 8 March 1887, sanction was given for the battalion to adopt the scarlet doublet with yellow facings and glengarry of the Argylls. From General Grierson's information it would seem that only the battalions mentioned wore the home service helmet, the remaining four being content with the shako, glengarry or Kilmarnock bonnet.

Princess Victoria's (Royal Irish Fusiliers)
Late 87th (or Royal Irish Fusiliers) and 89th (The Princess Victoria's) Regiments

Kipling and King illustrate an officer's helmet plate to the 89th Regiment together with the following description: 'The Garter omitted. In the centre a circle inscribed *Princess Victoria's Regiment* and within this the Sphinx superscribed *Egypt* above the numerals *89*. Above the circlet, two scrolls inscribed *Java, Ava* and below the circle two scrolls inscribed *Niagara, Sevastopol*. All in gilt.' Upon becoming a fusilier regiment in 1881, the home service helmet was no longer used.

Queen's Own Cameron Highlanders

The regiment did not wear the home service helmet.

Queen's Own (Royal West Kent Regiment)
Late 50th (or the Queen's Own) and 97th (Earl of Ulster's) Regiments

Dress Regulations, 1883, 1891, 1894, 1900, 1904, 1911

On Helmet Plates: In silver, on a black velvet ground, the White Horse of Kent on a scroll inscribed Invicta. Above

the Horse, another scroll with motto Que fas et Gloria ducunt. On the universal scroll, 'The Royal West Kent Regiment.'

The White Horse of Kent and motto *Invicta* were introduced in 1881 and had been a former badge of the West Kent Militia. It had appeared on the pre-1881 50th Regiment officers' helmet plates together with a scroll inscribed 'Queen's Own' and a silver Sphinx superscribed 'Egypt'. The honour had been awarded to the 50th for its services in Egypt during the 1801 campaign. The other ranks helmet plate centres had the horse in white metal and the mottos in gilding metal. West Kent was on the circle.

Illustrations

290 A fine example of an officer's helmet with queen's crown helmet plate. Note how the chin strap has been connected to the hook at the back of the helmet.

291 Officer's helmet with king's crown plate.

292 Other ranks helmet plate centre.

293 In this unusual rear view of the regiment by Richard Simkin, we see two mounted officers leading a column wearing white foreign service helmets with home service helmet plates. The image is from Supplement No 86 of Richard Simkin's 'Military Types' series produced for the Army and Navy Gazette and published on 2 February 1895.

294 Home service helmet plates were worn on the white helmets used on overseas stations. Here we see an example of an officer's plate used that way; but strangely the white horse centre comes with no mottos and is actually facing the wrong way. Animals used on headdress badges are always required to face to the viewer's left, unless when used on the collar. The left badge in this case would face inwards and to the right.

295 An original watercolour by Harry Payne of a sergeant. Both Queen's and King's Medals for South Africa are being worn, the collar badge being the Royal Crest and an old badge of the 50th Regiment. (*Anne SK Brown Military Collection, Brown University Library*)

Queen's (Royal West Surrey Regiment)
Late 2nd (Queen's Royal) Regiment

Dress Regulations, 1883, 1891, 1894, 1900, 1904

    On Helmet Plates: On a scarlet velvet ground, the Paschal Lamb in silver. On the universal scroll 'The Royal West Surrey Regiment.'

Dress Regulations, 1911

On Helmet Plates: On a scarlet velvet ground, the Paschal Lamb in silver.
On the universal scroll 'The Royal West Surrey Regiment.' Above the Garter a silver scroll inscribed 'The Queen's.'

The origins of the regiment's Paschal Lamb badge is, as historians point out, obscure. Regimental tradition associates it, together with the original sea green facings worn, with Catherine of Braganza. But authorities on heraldry have found no connection between the badge and the Portuguese royalty. The device of a lamb (the 'Lamb of God'), of course, is much used as a religious symbol and thoughts along these lines suggest that it was appropriately adopted by the regiment upon going to fight against infidels in Tangier. Regulations for Clothing and Colours published in 1747, regardless of origin, give a lamb as the regiment's ancient badge. Indeed, the Colours in 1751 are recorded as having three lambs on a green ground. The lamb is shown carrying the flag of St George on a staff over its shoulder, which to some suggested a lance. Quite when the regiment acquired its 'Mutton Lancers' nickname is not known.

The Paschal Lamb was to feature in the centre of both the officers' and other ranks helmet plates, the officers sometime just prior to 1911 placing an additional scroll inscribed 'The Queen's' between the top of the Garter and crown. The circles inscribed 'West Surrey', the helmet plate centres of the other ranks were gilding metal with the lamb in white metal.

Illustrations

296 An officers' pattern Victorian crown helmet plate with silver lamb on a scarlet velvet ground and title scroll reading 'The Royal West Surrey Regiment', as directed by the Dress Regulations of 1900. (*Bruce Bassett-Powel and Bob Bennet*)

297 A post-1902 King's crown version of the officer's helmet plate.

298 An other ranks gilding metal helmet plate with silver lamb and Victorian crown.

299 By 1911, and the issue of the Dress Regulations for that year, an additional scroll inscribed 'The Queen's' had been placed at the top of the officers' helmet plates between the Garter and crown. (*Bruce Bassett-Powell and Bob Bennet*)

300 In an Edwardian barrack scene by artist Harry Payne, a mounted officer returns the salute of a sentry. All men are wearing blue home service helmets in the image. (*Anne SK Brown Military Collection, Brown University Library*)

301 Richard Simkin painted the regiment during the currency of the helmet, illustration (6) being published on 7 March 1891 and from his 'Military Types' series of supplements produced for the Army and Navy Gazette.

302 Formed in 1881 from the former 2nd Royal Surrey Militia, NCOs and privates of the 3rd Battalion are seen in this photograph taken at camp. All but one, who wears a forage cap, wear blue helmets with Victorian crown star plates and Paschal Lamb centres. (*Alan Seymour*)

303 The Queen's (Royal West Surrey Regiment) had four volunteer battalions. Formed out of the former 2nd, 4th, 6th and 8th Surrey Rifle Volunteer Corps, all wore the helmet. In this illustration we see a private of the Croydon-based 1st Volunteer Battalion who wears a green uniform with scarlet facings. The helmet has a star-pattern Queen's crown plate with Lamb device in the centre.

304 Bermondsey was the headquarters of the 3rd Volunteer Battalion, a member of which can be seen here wearing a scarlet jacket with blue facings. The helmet is blue and has a white metal Victorian star plate.

305 Photographed by W Gregory & Co of the Strand in London, three members of the 4th Volunteer Battalion (headquarters at 71 New Street, Kennington Park) wearing Maltese Cross type plates with the Paschal Lamb as a centre piece on their green helmets. Note how the officer on the right, who is dressed for riding, has exchanged the spike on his helmet for a ball.

306 The actual helmet plate being worn in illustration 305.

307 Artist Richard Caton Woodville's watercolour representing the Territorials of the Queen's (Royal West Surrey Regiment) includes three officers and a regimental quartermaster sergeant. All wear green uniforms with scarlet facings, black patent leather belts and Pascal Lamb badges. Clearly seen on the pouch of the officer with his back to the viewer is the device of a crown over a bugle-horn. A fourth officer, mounted on the far left, is from the Royal Army Medical Corps. Note how the artist has been careful to show his helmet with a ball in lieu of the usual spike. The illustrated is the original artwork provided by the artist for His Majesty's Territorial Army by Walter Richards.

308 A drummer of the regiment by Frederick Stansell from WJ Gordon's book, Bands of the British Army.

Rifle Brigade (The Prince Consort's Own)

Dress Regulations, 1883

On Helmet Plates: In bronze, an eight-pointed star; on the star, a wreath of laurel intertwined with a scroll bearing the battles of the Brigade. Within the wreath, a Maltese cross, with a Lion between each division. On each division, other battles of the Brigade. On the centre, a circle inscribed 'Rifle Brigade;' within the circle, a bugle with strings, surmounted by the Crown. Above the cross, a crown on a tablet, inscribed 'Waterloo;' below the cross, a scroll, inscribed 'Peninsula,' and another, on the bottom of the wreath, inscribed 'The Prince Consort's Own.' The dimensions of the star, measured at the back, are from top to bottom, 5½ inches; width 4¼ inches.

Dress Regulations, 1891

On Helmet Plates: In bronze, a wreath of laurel intertwined with a scroll bearing the battles of the Brigade. Within a Maltese cross, with a Lion between each division. On each division, other battles of the Brigade. On the centre, a circle inscribed 'Rifle Brigade;'

Illustrations

309 Although Dress Regulations for 1891 still referred to the helmet plate, the brigade had in fact changed to the more rifle-like busby the year before. This illustration shows the star type plate mentioned in 1883. (*Bruce Bassett-Powell and Bob Bennet*)

310 The 1891 version of the officers' helmet plate. (*Bruce Bassett-Powell and Bob Bennet*)

311 Colour plate after Artists Auguste Legras. (*Anne SK Brown Military Collection, Brown University Library*)

312 Colour plate after Richard Simkin. Signed and dated 1885, the painting also shows a rifleman who appears to be wearing a circular helmet plate similar to illustration 310. (*Anne SK Brown Military Collection, Brown University Library*)

within the circle, a bugle with strings, surmounted by the Crown. Above the cross, a crown on a tablet, inscribed 'Waterloo;' below the cross, a scroll, inscribed 'Peninsula,' and another, on the bottom of the wreath, inscribed 'The Prince Consort's Own.'

Royal Army Medical Corps

Dress Regulations, 1883

    Helmet plate: Under Army Hospital Corps, As for Infantry of the Line; in the centre a red Geneva cross, on a silver ground.

Dress Regulations. 1891

    Helmet plate: Under Army Medical Department, The Royal Arms in gilt metal.

Dress Regulations, 1894

    Helmet plate: Under Army Medical Staff, The Royal Arms in gilt metal.

Illustrations

313 Officers' Victorian crown helmet plate with Geneva cross centre. (*Bruce Bassett-Powell and Bob Bennet*)

314 Royal Arms type as described in Dress Regulations for 1891 and 1894. (*Bruce Bassett-Powell and Bob Bennet*)

315 Royal Arms type with 'Royal Army Medical Corps' title scroll. (*Bruce Bassett-Powell and Bob Bennet*)

316 Original watercolour painting by J McNeill showing helmets with king's crown star plates and ball fittings. *Anne SK Brown Military Collection, Brown University Library*)

317 Colour plate after Frank Feller showing an officer with Royal Arms helmet plate.

318 Colour plate after Richard Caton Woodville showing an officer of the Royal Army Medical Corps (*Territorial Force*).

319 Colour plate after Lieutenant-General Sir James Moncrieff Grierson of a private, Royal Army Medical Corps (*Volunteers*).

Dress Regulations, 1900
> *On the Helmet: The Royal Arms with a scroll below, inscribed 'Royal Army Medical Corps.'*

Dress Regulations, 1904
> *On the Helmet: The Royal Arms with a scroll below, inscribed 'Royal Army Medical Corps.' For the Militia, as above with 'M' in silver on lower part of badge.*

Dress Regulations, 1911
> *On the Helmet: The Royal Arms with a scroll below, inscribed 'Royal Army Medical Corps.'*

Royal Army Medical Corps (Volunteers) wore white metal star helmet plates and several are illustrated by Kipling and King. All with the Geneva cross, titles appear on either circles or straps: 'Volunteer Medical Staff Corps', 'Royal Army Medical Volunteers', 'Forth V.I.B. Bearer Company', 'Leic. & Linc. Vol. Bde. Bearer Company' and 'Liverpool (Vol) I.B. Bearer Brigade'

Royal Dublin Fusiliers

Late 102nd (Royal Madras Fusiliers) and 103rd (Royal Bombay Fusiliers) Regiments

Home service helmets not worn.

Royal Engineers

Dress Regulations, 1883, 1891, 1894
> *Helmet Plate: Gilt device – Royal Arms with scrolls and mottos 'Quo fas et Gloria ducunt' and 'Ubique.' Dimensions:- From top of crest to bottom of plate, back measurement, 3 7/8 inches. Extreme horizontal width, back measurement, 3 inches.*

Dress Regulations, 1900
> *On Helmet Plate: As for R.A., but with the gun omitted. For Royal Engineers Militia, as for Royal Engineers, but with 'Militia' added on a smaller scroll.*

Dress Regulations, 1904
> *Helmet Plate: As for R.A., but with the gun omitted. For Royal Engineers (Militia), but with 'M' added between the scrolls.*

Dress Regulations, 1911
> *Helmet Plate: The Royal Arms in gilt or gilding metal with mottos 'Ubique' and 'Quo fas et Gloria ducunt' on scrolls below.*

The Royal Arms, together with both mottos were authorized in 1832. For Militia helmet plates, Arthur L Kipling and Hugh L King record three examples in Volume One of their *Head-dress Badges of the British Army*. All are of the Royal Arms type: '1, Below the Royal Arms a scroll inscribed *Militia Engineers*. In gilt for officers and gilding metal for other-ranks.' '2, Similar to above but with a scroll engraved with a laurel-spray above the title scroll. In gilt for officers.' '3, Below the Royal Arms a scroll inscribed *Royal Engineers* with a laurel-spray in the centre and below this a further scroll inscribed *Militia*. In gilet for officers.'

Volunteer Engineer helmet plates were as the Regulars, but in white metal and without the word 'Ubique', the scroll either being left blank or engraved with a spray of laurel. The lower scrolls in most cases retained the motto, but version inscribed either 'Engineer Volunteers' or 'Engineer Volunteer' have been noted. Unit titles were also displayed, eg, '1st Bedfordshire' on the upper scroll, 'Royal Engineers Volunteers' on the lower. Daniel Brinson illustrates two helmet plates to Royal Engineer cadet units in his book *Military Insignia of Gloucestershire:* the Cheltenham College and Clifton College.

Illustrations

320 The officers' helmet plate described above.

321 Richard Simkin's Supplement No 33, published on 6 September 1890 with the Army and Navy Gazette.

322 1st Lanarkshire Engineer Volunteer Corps.

323 Four members, including a bandsmen, of the 2nd Gloucestershire Engineer Volunteer Corps from Bristol.

324 Quarter Master Sergeant WJ Edwards who served with the Royal Engineers Submarine Miners.

Royal Fusiliers (City of London) Regiment

Late 7th (or Royal Fusiliers) Regiment

The Regular battalions did not wear the home service helmet. In 1881 the Royal London Militia became a battalion of the regiment and Major HG Parkyn writes in 1936 (*Journal of the Society for Army Historical Research,* Volume 15) that the badge of the regiment, the arms of the City of London together with the motto *Domine dirige nos*, appeared on the helmet plates within a wreath of oak leaves. The author also notes, in the same article, that officers of the South Middlesex Militia, which became the 5th Battalion of the Royal Fusiliers in 1881, displayed the arms of the County of Middlesex (thee Saxon seaxes) but without the crown.

The Royal Westminster Militia provided the regiment's 3rd Battalion in 1881. An officer's star-type helmet plate can be seen in Kipling and King's book with the following description: 'An eight-pointed star, the topmost point displaced by a Victorian crown. On this a laurel-wreath and within this a circlet inscribed *3rd or Royal Westminster Middlesex*. In the centre a shield bearing on the left side the portcullis from the Arms of Westminster and on the right three seaxes from the Arms of Middlesex. The shield surmounted by a bugle with strings. Across the base of the wreath a scroll inscribed *Mediterraneon*. In white-metal.'

Royal Garrison Regiment

Formed in 1901, disbanded 1908.

Dress Regulations, 1904
   Helmet Plate: The Royal Arms.

Royal Guernsey Militia

A force of unpaid volunteers had existed in Guernsey as far back as 1203 when King John had issued an order directing that men and money should be raised to defend the island from any invasion. Upon the 50th anniversary of the 1781 Battle of Jersey in January 1831, William IV conferred the prefix 'Royal' in January 1831. The words 'Diex aïx', an ancient battle cry used by the Duke of Normandy, featured on the badges. The sprig of laurel and three lions-leopardés from the arms of Guernsey were also used. The Royal Guernsey Militia comprised an artillery regiment and three of light infantry, the 1st (East), 2nd (North) and 3rd (South).

Dress Regulations, 1883, 1891
   Helmet Plate: In gilt metal, a garter inscribed 'Pro aris, rege et focis.' In silver, within the garter, on a black velvet ground, a shield surmounted by a sprig of laurel. The shield charged with three lions-leopardés. In silver, above the garter, a scroll inscribed 'DIEX AÏE.' In silver, below the shield, a bugle with strings. Within the strings, the number of the regiment. On universal wreath at the bottom, a scroll inscribed, 'Royal Guernsey Militia.'

Dress Regulations, 1900, 1904
   Helmet Plate: The universal plate, with the Garter inscribed 'Pro aris, rege et focis.' In silver, within the Garter, on a black velvet ground, a shield charged with three lions-leopardés surmounted by a sprig of laurel; above the Garter, a scroll inscribed 'Diex Aïe' below the shield, a bugle with strings. Within the strings, the number of the regiment. On universal wreath at the bottom, a scroll inscribed, 'Royal Guernsey Militia.'

Dress Regulations, 1911
   Helmet Plate: A circle inscribed 'Pro aris, rege et focis is substituted for the Garter. On the circle, in silver on a black velvet ground, a shield charged with three

lions-leopardés surmounted by a sprig of laurel. Above the Garter, a scroll inscribed 'Diex Aïe.' Below the circle a bugle with strings. Within the strings, the battalion number. On the bottom of the universal wreath a scroll inscribed, 'Royal Guernsey Militia.'

Illustrations

325 - An officer's helmet plate to the 2nd Regiment, Kipling and King showing a king's crown version on page 137 of their book.

326 The other ranks helmet plate centre, Kipling and King giving the following description, 'On circlet: Royal Guernsey Light Infantry. In the centre: A shield bearing the Arms of Guernsey (three lions leopardés) surmounted by a sprig of laurel. Above the shield a scroll inscribed Diex Aie. All in gilding-metal'.

Royal Inniskilling Fusiliers

Late 27th (Inniskilling) and 108th (Madras Infantry) Regiments

Kipling and King illustrate an officer's helmet plate to the 27th Regiment together with the following description: 'On a red-velvet ground in silver the Castle of Inniskilling with St George's flag flying from the centre turret. Below, the numerals 27'. They also mention the following regarding an officer's plate to the 108th Regiment: 'The Garter omitted. Within the laurel-wreath a second wreath of laurel with, across the base of the wreath a scroll inscribed *Central India*. Within the wreath a strap inscribed *Madras Infantry* and in the centre the numerals 108.' Author RG Harris includes a photograph of a private of the 108th Regiment in his book, *The Irish Regiment a Pictorial History 1683-1987*. Taken at Portsmouth, the image shows the subject with a home service helmet, the star plate having '108' in the centre. On becoming a fusilier regiment in 1881, the helmet was not used.

Royal Irish Regiment

Late 18th (The Royal Irish) Regiment

Dress Regulations, 1883, 1891, 1894, 1900, 1904, 1911

On Helmet Plates: In silver, on a scarlet ground, the Harp and Crown within a wreath of shamrock. On the universal scroll 'The Royal Irish.'

On 20 August 1695, the regiment took part in the assault on the castle at Namur, a heroic attack after which King William was graciously pleased to confer the right to display the badge of the Harp and Crown and that of the Lion of Nassau together with the motto *Virtutis Namurcensis Præmium* (Reward for valour at Namur).

As indicated by Dress Regulations, the title scrolls on the officers' helmet plates changed from 'The Royal Irish' to 'The Royal Irish Regiment' and helmet plates exist with both. Kipling and King illustrate queen's and king's crown examples. Other ranks helmet plate centres had the crowned harp without shamrocks (both queen's and king's crown types exist) and 'Royal Irish' on the circle. An officer's helmet plate has been recorded to the Wexford Militia

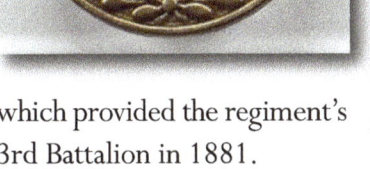

which provided the regiment's 3rd Battalion in 1881.

Illustrations

327 Officer's helmet plate with 'The Royal Irish' title scroll. (*Bruce Bassett-Powell and Bob Bennet*)

328 Officer's helmet with Victorian crown plate.

329 Other ranks helmet plate centre with post-1901 king's crown.

330 An original watercolour painting by Harry Payne featuring two signallers wearing king's crown helmet plates. The collar badges are the arms of Nassau which, together with the motto Virtutis Namurcensis Precemium, were conferred upon the regiment as a reward for the gallantry shown during the siege and assault of Namur in 1695. (*Anne SK Brown Military Collection, Brown University Library*)

331 Officer's helmet, Wexford Militia. Th 'XCIX' (99) represents the regiment's precedence within the Militia List.

Royal Irish Rifles

Late 83rd (County of Dublin) and 86th (Royal County Down) Regiments

Dress Regulations, 1883, 1891, 1894

On Helmet Plates: In bronze, a shamrock wreath intertwined with a scroll bearing the battles of the regiment; within the wreath, the Harp and Crown. Above the Harp, a scroll inscribed Quis separabit; between the Harp, the Sphinx over Egypt; below the Sphinx, a bugle with strings. Over the strings of the bugle, a scroll, inscribed 'Royal Irish Rifles.' No star behind.

The Sphinx superscribed 'Egypt' had been authorised as a badge to the 86th Regiment for its services during the campaign of 1801. The Harp and Crown, together with the motto *Quis separabit* was also from the 86th. The post-1881 officer's helmet plates were not of the universal crowned star type. Helmets were no longer worn after 1890.

In his book *The Irish Regiment a Pictorial History*, RG Harris shows a Maltese Cross plate to the County Louth Rifle Militia which in 1881 provided the regiment's 5th Battalion. The usual lions between the arms of the cross are absent and a blank tablet is placed between it and a Victorian crown. There is a harp in the centre of a circle inscribed 'County Louth Rifles'.

Illustration

332 Officer's helmet plate.

Royal Jersey Light Infantry

Dress Regulations, 1883, 1891, 1894

On Helmet Plate: In gilt metal, within a circle inscribed 'Royal Jersey Light Infantry,' a bugle with strings on a black velvet ground. The number of the regiment within the strings of the bugle.

Dress Regulations, 1900, 1904

Helmet Plate: On the universal plate circle inscribed 'Royal Jersey Light Infantry,' is substituted for the Garter. In the centre, in gilt or gilding metal, the bugle and strings; within the strings the number of the regiment.

Dress Regulations, 1911

Helmet Plate: A circle inscribed 'Royal Jersey Light Infantry,' is substituted for the Garter. In the centre, in gilt metal on a black velvet ground, a bugle and strings; within the strings the battalion numeral.

The other ranks helmet plate centre had a bugle, the circle being inscribed 'Royal Jersey Light Infantry'.

Illustration

333 Officer's Victorian helmet plate for 2nd Regiment. Kipling and King illustrate a king's crown version to the 3rd Regiment, but with a sprig of laurel above the bugle. (*Bruce Bassett-Powell and Bob Bennet*)

Royal Marine Artillery

Kipling and King illustrate and describe two helmet plates:

(1) 'Helmet-plate 1879-1905. Officers: A fused grenade with eighteen points to the flames and with a narrow neck. On the ball a laurel-wreath with, above, a scroll inscribed *Gibraltar* and with the 'Fouled Anchor' at the bottom-join of the wreath. Within the wreath a voided strap inscribed *Per mare per terram* and, in the centre, the Globe. Blue-enamel backing to the strap, the Globe in silver, remainder in gilt.'

(2) 'Helmet-plate: Officers' 1879-1905; Other-ranks, 1879 to 1923. Officers: A fused grenade with nine points to the flames and with a wide neck. Other details as per previous pattern. Blue-enamel backing to the strap, the Globe in silver-and-gilt, remainder in gilt.'

Illustrations

334 Officers helmet plate with eighteen flame grenade. (*Bruce Bassett-Powell and Bob Bennet*)

335 Officer's helmet.

Royal Marine Light Infantry

For the officers' Victorian crown helmet plate, Kipling and King give the following description: 'An eight-pointed star, the topmost point displaced by a Victorian crown. On this a laurel-wreath and within that a voided strap inscribed *Per mare per terram*. In the centre the Globe. Above the strap a scroll inscribed *Gibraltar*. On the bottom-join of the wreath the Fouled Anchor and below this a bugle with strings. Blue-enamel backing to the strap, the Globe and bugle in silver, remainder in gilt.'

The authors also mention the other ranks pattern: 'Similar in design to the officers' pattern but the motto is on a circlet instead of a strap and the Fouled Anchor at the base is superimposed on the strings of the bugle. In gilding-metal.'

Illustrations

336 Officers' helmet plate. (*Bruce Bassett-Powell and Bob Bennet*)

337 Colour plate after Richard Simkin.

338 Sheet music cover with artwork from Frank Dadd. (*Anne SK Brown Military Collection, Brown University Library*)

339 Officers' helmet and carrying tin.

Royal Military Academy

Illustrated by Kipling and King with the following description: 'An eight-pointed star the topmost point displaced by a Victorian crown. On this a gilt laurel-wreath. Within the wreath a gilt pierced strap inscribed *Nec aspera terrent* with a blue-enamel ground. In the centre the Royal Cypher *VR* in gilt on a red-enamel ground'.

Royal Military College Sandhurst

Established at Great Marlow as a training facility for officers of cavalry, infantry and the departmental corps in 1802, the college moved to a permanent home at Sandhurst in 1812.

Dress Regulations, 1883

Hemet: For Adjutant and Quartermaster, In gilt metal a star surmounted by the crown; on the star a laurel wreath; within the wreath a garter pierced 'Nec aspera terrent,' the ground of blue enamel. In the centre of the garter on a ground of red enamel, the Royal Cypher in gilt metal.

Dress Regulations, 1891, 1894

Hemet: For Quartermasters, In gilt metal a star surmounted by the crown; on the star a laurel wreath; within the wreath a garter pierced 'Nec aspera terrent,' the ground of blue enamel. In the centre of the garter on a ground of red enamel, the Royal Cypher in gilt metal.

Dress Regulations, 1900

On Full Dress Head-dress: None worn. The entry includes a note to say that the Quartermaster wears badge as for the Field Cap.

Kipling and King illustrate a plate for officer cadets on page 273, item 1070. Dated 1881-1901, the description given is as follows: 'A gilt eight-pointed star the topmost point displaced by a Victorian crown. On this a gilt laurel-wreath. Within the wreath a gilt pierced strap inscribed *Nec aspera terrent* with a blue-enamel ground. In the centre the Royal Cypher *VR* in gilt on a red-enamel ground.'

Illustrations
340 A fine specimen of a helmet. (*Stuart Bates*)
341 The helmet plate.

Royal Munster Fusiliers
Late 101st (Royal Bengal Fusiliers) and 104th (Bengal Fusiliers) Regiments

Home service helmet not worn.

Royal Regiment of Artillery

Dress Regulations, 1883

Helmet Plate: Gilt, device – the Royal Arms with gun below. 'Ubique' above the gun and 'Quo fas et Gloria ducunt' below.

Dress Regulations, 1891

Field and Garrison Artillery, and Coast Brigade. Helmet Plate: Gilt, device – the Royal *Arms* with gun below. 'Ubique' above the gun and 'Quo fas et Gloria ducunt' below. Dimensions – From top of crest to bottom of plate, back measurement, 3 7/8 inches. Extreme horizontal width, back measurement, 3 inches. For Militia Artillery, 'Ubique' omitted, and the designation of the county to which the regiment belongs substituted for 'Quo fas et Gloria ducunt,' or in the case of the Channel Islands Artillery Militia, the name of the regiment as 'Royal Jersey Artillery.'

Royal Malta Artillery: Helmet Plate, special pattern.

Dress Regulations, 1894

Field and Garrison Artillery: Gilt, device—the Royal Arms with gun below. 'Ubique' above the gun and 'Quo fas et Gloria ducunt' below.

Dress Regulations, 1900

On Helmet Plate: In gilt or gilding metal. The Royal Arms with gun below. 'Ubique' above, and 'Quo fas et Gloria ducunt' below the gun. The description begins by pointing out that this type of plate is not worn by the Royal Horse Artillery. For the Royal Artillery Militia, the Regulations give: *The letter M, in silver, is added below the gun and above the bottom scroll.* Also mentioned is the Royal Malta Artillery as follows: *Within a wreath surmounted by a crown, the Garter inscribed 'Royal Malta Artillery.' Within the Garter the Maltese Cross. The gun below the wreath.*

Dress Regulations, 1904

On Helmet Plate: In gilt or gilding metal. The Royal Arms with gun below. 'Ubique' above, and 'Quo fas et Gloria ducunt' below the gun. Not worn by R.H.A. For Royal Artillery (Militia), The Royal Arms with the letter M, in silver, added below the gun and above the bottom scroll.

Dress Regulations, 1911

On Helmet Plate: Of gilt or gilding metal, the Royal Arms with gun below; the gun surmounted by a scroll inscribed 'Ubique', the motto 'Quo fas et Gloria ducunt' below.

Units of the Volunteer Artillery were required to have the 'Ubique' scroll either left blank, or displaying a laurel spray. The bottom, '*Quo fas et Gloria ducunt*' scroll was often changed to reflect the title of the corps. Some plates had on the lower scroll 'Artillery Volunteers' or, after 1891, 'Volunteer Artillery'. The different helmet plates worn number in their hundreds and for a comprehensive account I must refer you to *The Volunteer Artillery 1859-1908* by Norman Lichfield and Ray Westlake.

Territorial artillery units formed in 1908 took into use helmet plates which retained the laurel spray on the upper scroll, but showed the original motto on the lower. Territorial Artillery insignia is comprehensively dealt with by Norman Lichfield's book on the subject. Captain RJ Macdonald records in his superb book, *The History of the Dress of the Royal Regiment of Artillery,* how the 'Cork helmet for Officers of Garrison and Field Artillery, covered with blue cloth, with gilt spike [replaced by a ball in 1881]' was introduced in 1878.

Illustrations

342 From Captain RJ Macdonald's *The History of the Dress of the Royal Regiment of Artillery*, first published by Henry Sotheran & Co in 1899, a colour plate dated 1897 which shows two officers, one mounted, the other dismounted. Both are wearing helmets with ball fittings and gilt plates.

343 For the Tuck series of postcards, 'Regimental Badges and their Wearers', artist Harry Payne produced the detailed study of an officer.

344 Victorian crown example of the officers' helmet plate. (Bruce Bassett-Powell, Bob Bennet)

345 Orkney Artillery Volunteers.

346 1st Cheshire and Carnarvon.

347 Photograph by Gregory & Co of the Strand, London of five members of the 1st West Riding of Yorkshire Volunteer Artillery.

348 Territorial Force artillery units formed in 1908 took into use helmet plates which retained the laurel spray on the upper scroll, but showed the original motto on the lower.

349 Members of the Hampshire Royal Garrison Artillery Volunteers, some wearing the full-dress helmet with service dress.

350 Officer's helmet with a spray of laurel replacing 'Ubique' and 'Volunteer Artillery' on the lower scroll. (*Stuart Bates*)

351 Officer's helmet with carrying tin.

352 1st Essex Artillery Volunteer Corps. (*Michael Wood*)

353 Other ranks helmet, 1st Essex Artillery Volunteer Corps.

Royal Scots Fusiliers

Late 21st (Royal Scots Fusiliers) Regiment

The regular battalions did not wear the home service helmet. Forming a volunteer battalion of the Royal Scots Fusiliers in 1881, the 1st Roxburgh and Selkirk (The Border) Rifle Volunteer Corps had adopted grey helmets with bronze Maltese Cross on a black ground in 1879. The battalion transferred to the King's Royal Rifle Corps in 1887.

Illustration

354 Colour plate by Lieutenant-General Sir James Moncrieff Grierson showing a captain (1879-1902) and a private (1902-1907).

Royal Scots (Lothian Regiment)
late 1st (The Royal Scots Regiment)

Dress Regulations, 1883

On Helmet Plates: The Garter and universal wreath are omitted. The Star of the Order of the Thistle, in gilt metal. On the star, a silver circle, pierced Nemo me impune lacessit; the ground of green enamel. Within the circle, on a convex ground of green enamel, the Thistle, in silver. On the universal scroll 'The Lothian Regt.'

Dress Regulations, 1891, 1894

On Helmet Plates: The Garter and universal wreath are omitted. The Star of the Order of the Thistle, in gilt metal. On the star, a silver circle, pierced Nemo me impune lacessit; the ground of green enamel. Within the circle, on a convex ground of green enamel, the Thistle, in silver. On the universal scroll 'The Royal Scots.'

Dress Regulations, 1900

On Helmet Plates: The Garter and universal wreath are omitted. The Star of the Order of the Thistle, in gilt or gilding metal. On the star, a silver circle, pierced Nemo me impune lacessit; the ground of green enamel. Within the circle, on a convex ground of green enamel, the Thistle, in silver. On the universal scroll 'The Royal Scots.'

Dress Regulations, 1904

On Helmet Plates: Not worn.

The Star of the Order of the Thistle, the figure of St Andrew with his Cross and the motto *Nemo me impune lacessit* (None may touch me with impunity) are all ancient badges of the regiment. The Sphinx superscribed 'Egypt' would also make an appearance on the helmet plates worn by other ranks, this honour dating back to the campaign of 1801.

Lawrence Weaver in his book *The Story of The Royal Scots* (Country Life, London, 1915) shows a rough sketch of the officers' helmet plate worn for the period 1878-1881 and makes the following comment: 'Chacos disappeared in 1878 in favour of the blue helmet, and gave the military tailors the chance to alter helmet-plates with considerable frequency.' Certainly, this was true.

The first helmet plate to be worn by officers, and that sketched by Lawrence Weaver, can be seen on the dustjacket of Volume One of *Head-dress Badges of the British Army* by Arthur L Kipling and Hugh L King. One of the most attractive helmet plates ever produced, the authors give the following description: 'The Garter omitted. Within the laurel-wreath the Collar of the Order of the Thistle with St Andrew and

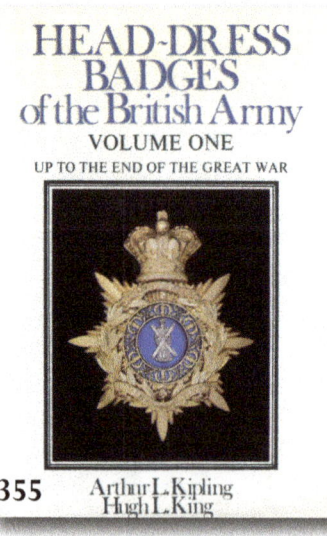
355 Arthur L Kipling Hugh L King

356

357

Cross in the centre. A scroll above inscribed *The Royal Scots* and a scroll below inscribed *Nemo me impune lacessit*. All gilt except St Andrew which is silver. A blue enamel ground to St Andrew and the Collar of the Order of the Thistle.' Noticeable is the absence of the universal Garter and regimental numbers that were a feature of most other regiments between 1878-1881.

358

Following in 1881 came an officers' plate which included the regiment's original title, that of the 'Lothian Regiment', on the silver title scroll. Soon another version would appear with 'The Royal Scots' instead. Other ranks helmet plate centres featuring St Andrew with his Cross, the motto *Nemo me impune lacessit* and a Sphinx superscribed 'Egypt', would also change; first with a 'Lothian' circle, followed by one with 'Royal Scots'. Next, the device that would become the regiment's most recognisable cap badge for many years to come—the Star of the Order of the Thistle with, in the centre, St Andrew and Cross. Below this, a scroll inscribed 'The Royal Scots'.

359

Lieutenant-General Sir James Moncrieff Grierson in his *Records of the Scottish Volunteer Force 1859-1908*, tells how the former 2nd Edinburgh Rifle Volunteer Corps had become the 4th Volunteer Battalion Royal Scots by Army Order 144 of 1 April 1888 and accordingly in that year had adopted the uniform of the regiment, wearing the helmet with it until 1904 when the Kilmarnock bonnet was introduced for officers and the glengarry became the sole head-dress for other ranks. The 1st Midlothian Rifle Volunteer Corps, which became the 5th Volunteer Battalion in 1888, wore a blue helmet from 1878 which had a rampant lion device on a silver star plate. In 1890 the uniform of the Royal Scots was adopted, and with it the helmet until June 1905.

Sometime during the early 1980s I was fortunate enough to find two helmet plates belonging to the volunteer corps of the County of Midlothian. The first was a magnificent specimen of an officer's plate to the 5th Volunteer Battalion Royal Scots. Of the pattern shown in illustration 357 below, it varied in as much as it had a king's crown. The star backplate was in silver, as was the Star of the Order of the Thistle. In gilt was the pierced circle and thistle and, as before, the background was of green enamel. An additional title scroll reading '5th Volunteer Battalion' was placed below that inscribed 'The Royal Scots'. Both were in gilt.

Referring to the two Midlothian helmet plates mentioned above, the second was to serve as a good example of how badges were sometimes adapted by volunteer corps to suite changes in title and style. In white metal, my second item was an other ranks helmet plate similar to the regular's pattern shown at illustration 359 below. There was, however, an additional scroll placed above St Andrew which read '6th Vol. Batt.' This would, of course, date the badge as post-1886. But, save for the centre piece, this would not turn out to be an entirely new badge to coincide with a change of title and uniform. Instead, the removal of the centre revealed that beneath was a one-piece, white metal, universal plate, the centre of which was as shown at illustration 358 below, minus the Sphinx. Inscribed on the circle was the title '2nd Midlothian & Peebles R.V.' Two holes had been punched to take the north and south lugs of the post 1886 badge. Images of the badges can be seen in my article, 'Three Helmet Plates of the Midlothian Rifle Volunteers'

which appeared in *The Bulletin of the Military Historical Society,* No 131, February 1983.

Illustrations

355 The cover of *Head-dress Badges of the British Army, Volume* 1 by Arthur L Kipling and Hugh L King. Featured is the first officers' helmet plate with its gilt, silver and blue enamel.

356 - In 1904 the regiment ceased to wear the helmet and instead took into use the more Scottish in appearance, Kilmarnock bonnet. But before this change, two patterns of officers' helmet plate would be worn. The year 1881 saw the introduction of a plate which again omitted the universal wreath and, as before, the Garter. Instead, a silver thistle within the centre of a circle bearing the Nemo me impune lacessit motto has replaced St Andrew, the circle then resting on a large Star of the Order of the Thistle which almost covers the whole of the universal backplate. The silver title scroll reads 'The Lothian Regt.' (*Bruce Bassett-Powell and Bob Bennet*)

357 The second post-1881 officers' helmet, much the same as that shown in illustration 356, but now with 'The Royal Scots' title scroll as directed in Dress Regulations for 1891.

358 The original other ranks helmet plate centres displayed the Star of the Order of the Thistle, the motto and a Sphinx superscribed 'Egypt' within a circle inscribed 'Lothian'. Worn from 1882 to 1889 was the same pattern, but with 'The Royal Scots' on the circle.

359 The third other ranks helmet plate, the centre now also to serve as a glengarry cap badge.

360 For his Supplement No 38, issued with the Army and Navy Gazette on 7 February 1891, artist Richard Simkin chose a group of three from the regiment: a piper, private and officer. Both the private and officer are wearing white foreign service helmets with star plates. The painting is signed and dated 1890.

361 General Grierson's records refer to the 2nd Midlothian and Peebles Rifle Volunteer Corps adopting blue helmets in 1886. Two years later it became the 6th Volunteer Battalion Royal Scots, retaining the helmet until 1900. The general's colour plate shows a lance-corporal for the period 1888-1900.

Royal Sussex Regiment

Late 35th (Royal Sussex) and 107th (Bengal Infantry Regiments)

Dress Regulations, 1883

On Helmet Plate: On a black velvet ground, badge as for collar but larger [A Maltese Cross, in gilt or gilding metal, on a feather in silver; on the cross a wreath in silver and green enamel; on the wreath the Garter and motto in blue enamel set with silver. Within the circle the Cross of St George in red enamel, set with silver, on a silver ground]. On the universal scroll 'The Royal Sussex Regiment.'

Dress Regulations, 1891, 1894

On Helmet Plate: On a black velvet ground, badge as for collar but larger [A Maltese Cross, in gilt or gilding metal, on a feather in silver; on the cross a wreath in silver and green enamel; on the wreath the Garter and motto in blue enamel set with silver. Within the circle the Cross of St George in red enamel, set with silver, on a silver ground] but larger. On the universal scroll 'The Royal Sussex Regiment.'

Dress Regulations, 1900

On Helmet Plate: On a black velvet ground, badge as for collar [A Maltese Cross, in gilt or gilding metal, on a feather in silver; on the cross a wreath in silver and green enamel; on the wreath the Garter and motto in blue enamel set with silver. Within the circle the Cross of St George in red enamel, set with silver, on a silver ground]. On the universal scroll 'The Royal Sussex Regiment.'

Dress Regulations, 1904

On Helmet Plate: On a red velvet ground, badge as for collar [A Maltese Cross, in gilt or gilding metal, on a feather in silver; on the cross a wreath in silver and green enamel; on the wreath the Garter and motto in blue enamel set with silver. Within the circle the Cross of St George in red enamel, set with silver, on a silver ground]. On the universal scroll 'The Royal Sussex Regiment.'

Dress Regulations, 1911

On Helmet Plate: On a scarlet velvet ground, badge as for collar [A Maltese Cross, in gilt or gilding metal, on a feather in silver; on the cross a wreath in silver and green enamel; on the wreath the Garter and motto in blue enamel set with silver. Within the circle the Cross of St George in red enamel, set with silver, on a silver ground]. On the universal scroll 'The Royal Sussex Regiment.'

A feature of the 35th Regiment's badges was the Roussillon plume, worn since 1759 but not officially authorised until June 1880. It is said that this distinction was in memory of Quebec when the men of the regiment took the white plumes from the dead of the French Royal Roussillon Grenadiers. Thought to commemorate the capture of Malta in 1800, a Maltese Cross appears on several of the regiment's badges and appointments, and from the old Royal Sussex Militia, the Star of the Order of the Garter. The other ranks helmet plate centres are described by Kipling and King as follows: 'On circlet: *Royal Sussex*. In centre: A Maltese cross, on this the Garter proper and, in the centre, St George's Cross. The whole surrounded by a laurel-wreath and with the Roussillon plume behind. All in gilding metal.'

An article published in the August 1971 edition of *The Bulletin of the Military Historical Society* tells how 'When the Cardwell System was introduced in 1881 the 1st Cinque Ports R.V.C. were allowed to retain their title and grey uniform.' The writer, who is not named, goes on to say, 'The shako was worn until 1885 and a dark green glengarry was then worn until the issue of a grey helmet in 1887. The helmet plate was a Maltese cross with a lion between the divisions of the cross and surmounted by a crown. On this a circlet inscribed "Cinque Ports Volunteers" with in the centre a bugle with strings and the numeral "1" within the strings.'

Also to appear in the MHS *Bulletin*, this time in February 1986, was the first of a series of articles on the Sussex Volunteers and Territorials by PJR Mileham. One of the photographs included with the item is of a group of 1st Volunteer Battalion officers wearing helmets with star plates, taken outside the Royal Pavilion, Brighton c1895.

Still with the Military Historical Society, its *Bulletin* for August 2010 includes a six-page comprehensive article on the Hurstpierpoint College Cadet Force. Staff and senior boys had been associated with the 13th Sussex Rifle Volunteer Corps since its formation in 1860. A cadet corps was formed and affiliated to the 2nd Volunteer Battalion at the college in in 1887. Written by Tim Wright, the article mentions how in June 1892, 'Full dress tunics (scarlet with blue facings at a cost of 16s each) and blue helmets with white metal spikes, helmet plates and chin chains were ordered.' 'The cadets', continues the author, 'would thus be dressed identically to the rest of the 2nd VB.'

Illustrations

362 Although the several editions of Dress Regulations give the spelling of 'Regiment' in full, the officer's helmet plate illustrated shows it abbreviated as 'Regt.'. Kipling and King suggest that this preceded the 'Regiment' version. But even the post-1901 king's crown pattern appears with the shortened 'Regt.' (*Bruce Bassett-Powell and Bob Bennet*)

363 Officer's helmet with king's crown plate and 'Regt.' on the title scroll.

364 One of the colour plates by artist Frank Feller used in Walter Richards's 1890s publication, Her Majesty's Army.

365 With the full 'Regiment' spelling, an officer's, king's crown helmet plate to the 1st Volunteer Battalion.

Royal Warwickshire Regiment

Late 6th (Royal First Warwickshire) Regiment

Dress Regulations, 1883, 1891, 1894

On Helmet Plates: On a black velvet ground, the Antelope, in silver, with gilt collar and chain. On the universal scroll 'The Royal Warwickshire Regiment.'

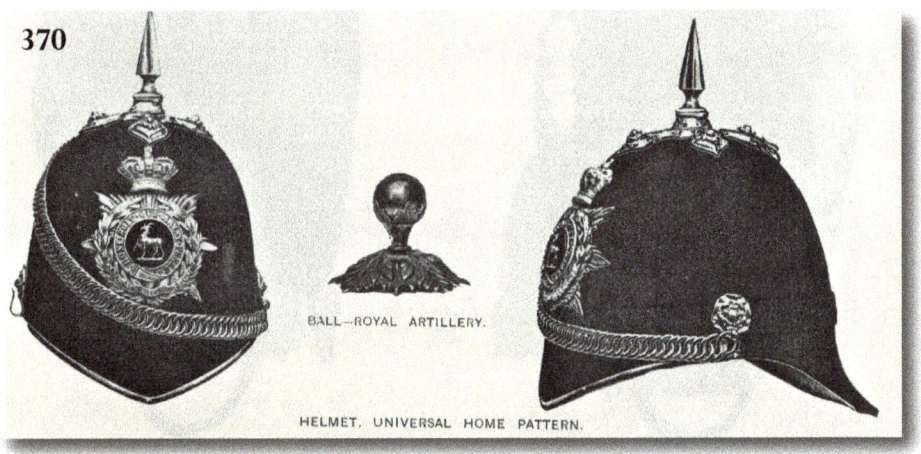

Dress Regulations, 1900, 1904, 1911

On Helmet Plates: On a black velvet ground, the Antelope, in silver, with gilt or gilding metal collar and chain. On the universal scroll 'The Royal Warwickshire Regiment.'

The Antelope was an ancient badge of the regiment and for many years in use on caps, breast-belt plates and buttons. The first officers' helmet plate displayed the Antelope above the Roman numerals 'VI'. The post-1881 other ranks brass helmet plate centres had 'Warwickshire' on the circle and the Antelope in white metal.

Illustrations

366 The post-1881 officers' helmet plate, gilt with silver antelope on a black velvet ground, gilt collar and silver title scroll. (*Bruce Bassett-Powell and Bob Bennet*)

367 The king's crown officers' helmet plate.

368 From Richard Simkin, an original watercolour of an officer who is shown with silver Antelope collar badges. (*Anne SK Brown Military Collection, Brown University Library*)

369 From Gale & Polden, a postcard featuring the work of Arthur Chidley. Here we have a drum major and bass drummer, both men wearing the chin straps of their helmets hooked up at the back.

370 In the photographic section of the 1900 Dress Regulations for Officers, a helmet with Royal Warwickshire Regiment plate was used as an example. The chin strap has been shown hooked up to the rear of the headdress.

371 From Colonel Charles J Hart's magnificent history of the 1st Volunteer Battalion (published by the Midland Counties Herald Ltd, Birmingham in 1906) we have an illustration which shows the uniform of the battalion in 1906. The uniform is dark grey with red facings and piping, the Maltese Cross helmet plate having a red cloth centre. Formally the 1st Warwickshire Rifle Volunteer Corps, headquarters of the battalion were in Thorpe Street, Birmingham.

372 Much of the old 3rd Warwickshire Rifle Volunteer Corps had been recruited from staff and senior boys at Rugby

School. A cadet corps was formed there in 1873 which would later be affiliated to the 2nd Volunteer Battalion Royal Warwickshire Regiment. One of the cadet corps is shown in this illustration. His blue cloth-covered headdress has a white metal universal-pattern, other ranks helmet plate with the Queen Victoria crown. The centre circle has the designation 2nd V.B. Royal Warwickshire Regiment. An antelope forms the central device. Note the Bear and Ragged Staff collar badges.

Royal Welsh Fusiliers

Late 23rd (Royal Welch Fusiliers) Regiment

The home service helmet was not worn

School of Musketry

Kipling and King show both queen's and king's crown versions. Of the universal crowned star, wreath and Garter type in gilding metal, crossed rifles appear in the centre.

Illustration

373 A king's crown plate.

Seaforth Highlanders
(Ross-shire Buffs, The Duke of Albany's)

The home service helmet was not worn by the regular battalions. The shakos of the 1st Administrative Battalion of Sutherland Rifle Volunteers gave way to blue helmets in 1879. Lieutenant-General Grierson record in his book, *Records of the Scottish Volunteer Force 1859-1908,* that the badge worn on the helmet was a 'star and crown in silver.' The battalion was consolidated as the 1st Sutherland Rifle Volunteer Corps in 1880 and in the following year entered the Army List as a volunteer battalion (without change of title) of the Seaforth Highlanders.

In 1860 the several rifle volunteer companies then in existence within the county of Elgin, were organised into an administrative battalion. Blue helmets were introduced in 1879 and in the following year the battalion was consolidated as the 1st Elgin Rifle Volunteer Corps. This became the 3rd Volunteer Battalion Seaforth Highlanders in 1887, the helmets being replaced by glengarry caps the year before.

Illustration

374 Colour plate from General Grierson's book, Records of the Scottish Volunteer Force, showing the several uniforms worn by the 3rd Volunteer Battalion Seaforth Highlanders and its predecessors.

Sherwood Foresters (Nottinghamshire and Derbyshire Regiment)
Late 45th (Nottinghamshire Sherwood Foresters) and 95th (The Derbyshire) Regiments

Dress Regulations, 1883, 1891, 1894

On Helmet Plates: In the helmet-plate, the Garter, with motto, is omitted. Within the universal wreath, a Maltese Cross, in silver. On the cross, in gilt metal, an oak-leaf wreath; within the wreath, on a ground of silver blue enamel, a Stag lodged, in silver. In gilt metal, on the left division of the cross, the word 'The'; on the right division, 'Regt.' and on a scroll on the lower division, 'Derbyshire.' A scroll of special pattern on the bottom of the universal wreath inscribed 'Sherwood Foresters.'

Dress Regulations, 1900

On Helmet Plates: In the helmet-plate, the Garter, with motto, is omitted. Within the universal wreath, a Maltese Cross, in silver. On the cross, in gilt or gilding metal, an oakleaf wreath; within the wreath, on a ground of silver blue enamel, a Stag lodged, in silver. In gilt or gilding metal, on the left division of the cross, the word 'The'; on the right division, 'Regt.' and on a scroll on the lower division, 'Derbyshire.' A scroll of special pattern on the bottom of the universal wreath inscribed 'Sherwood Foresters.'

Dress Regulations, 1904, 1911

On Helmet Plates: In the helmet-plate, the Garter, with motto, is omitted. Within the universal wreath, a Maltese Cross, in silver. On the cross, in gilt or gilding metal, an oakleaf wreath; within the wreath, on a ground of silver blue enamel, a Stag lodged, in silver. In gilt or gilding metal, on the left division of the cross, the word 'The'; on the right division, 'Regt.' and on a scroll on the lower division, 'Notts and Derby.' A scroll of special pattern on the bottom of the universal wreath inscribed 'Sherwood Foresters.'

Henry Manners Chichester and George Burgs-Short in their book, *The Records and Badges of Every Regiment and Corps in the British Army*, state that when raised, there were in the 95th Regiment many officers and men of the old 95th (later Rifle Brigade) and with this in mind, the Maltese Cross was taken into use as a badge. However, as Major HG Parkyn points out, there is no evidence to support this claim. A Stag lodged was an old badge of the Derbyshire Militia, taken from the arms of Derby.

The pre-1881 officers' helmet plate to the 45th Regiment is illustrated and described by Kipling and King on page 111 of their book—'On a red-velvet ground the numerals *45* in gilt. Beneath the Garter, in silver, a scroll inscribed *Sherwood Foresters*.' Other ranks helmet plate centres after 1881 have the Maltese Cross surmounted by a crown and the stag lodged within a wreath of oak leaves. The words, 'Sherwood', 'Foresters' and 'Derbyshire' were inscribed separately on three arms of the cross. The name on the circle was 'Derbyshire'. Both queen's and king's crown versions exist, as well as a post-1902 centre with the name 'Notts & Derby'.

In 1992 I was fortunate enough to see a copy of the Dress Regulations issued to members of the 1st Volunteer Battalion. Under 'Officers Full Dress' it noted, 'Helmet, tunic, waist sash, with white sword slings worn under the tunic...' The entry for NCOs and men also mentioned that the helmet was to be worn in full dress.

Illustrations
375 A fine example of an officers' gilt helmet plate with its blue enamel

centre, silver Maltese Cross and 'Sherwood Foresters' title scroll. (*Bruce Bassett-Powell and Bob Bennet*)

376 Gale & Polden postcard entitled 'Relieving the Sentry' featuring a corporal and two privates wearing king's crown helmet plates. Artist, Ernest Ibbetson.

377 From a Gale & Polden postcard set, a squad are seen being instructed in bayonet drill as an officer and sergeant talk in the near distance. Artist, Ernest Ibbetson.

378 Another postcard from the Aldershot company of Gale & Polden. A busy scene as with officers deep in conversation. A bugler tends the commanding officer's mount as he talks with the regimental sergeant major.

379 In this image by Richard Simkin a bugler in the far distance sounds a call as a colour-sergeant reports to an officer. Produced for the Army and Navy Gazette and published on 1 September 1894, this print is from Simkin's 'Military Types' series. Painted in the 1890s, Richard Simkin has given the regiment white facings, this being the required colour for an English Regiment after the 1881 reorganisations. The old green of the 45th Regiment, as seen in illustrations 2, 3 and 4, was, however, restored in 1913.

380 From the Nottingham studio of photographer EA Carnell, a portrait of a member of the 1st Nottinghamshire (Robin Hood) Rifle Volunteer Corps. The grey helmet has a Maltese Cross plate with the reverses and intertwined letters 'RHR' in the centre.

381 1st Volunteer Battalion.

South Staffordshire Regiment

Late 38th (1st Staffordshire) and 80th (Staffordshire Volunteers) Regiments

Dress Regulations, 1883, 1891, 1894, 1900, 1904, 1911

On Helmet Plates: In silver, on a black velvet ground, the Sphinx over Egypt. On the universal scroll, 'The South Staffordshire Regiment.'

The Sphinx superscribed 'Egypt' had been awarded to the 80th Regiment for its services during the campaign of 1801. The Stafford Knot is a device used by both the 38th and 80th Regiments. Kipling and King record the pre-1881 officers' star helmet plates, that for the 38th having the numerals '38' in the centre and a Stafford Knot in silver below the Garter. The 80th had the numerals in gilt on a black velvet ground. In May 1971, the *Bulletin of the Military Historical Society* published an interesting article entitled, 'The Staffords and the Stafford Knot'. Written by Colonel HCB Cook, the item mentions how in 1880 the 38th had removed the knot from their helmet plates. Conflicting with the Kipling and King account, Colonel Cook states that the 80th in fact had its number in Roman numerals, i.e. 'LXXX' within the Garter, 'but added a knot above it in 1880.' For the other ranks, the Sphinx superscribed 'Egypt' was in white metal, the circle being inscribed 'South Staffordshire'.

In the centre of the several badges worn by the King's Own Stafford Militia appears a castle-type structure complete with a flag flying from a single tower. A castle, not unusual as a device incorporated into a regimental badge in reference to its geographical association, but in the case of the King's Own this is not a fortification of any Staffordshire town. Impressed with the regiment's appearance and conduct after an inspection in 1797, King George III requested that the Staffordshire Militia be sent to Windsor to take up Royal duties. A comfortable billet indeed, not only for the year 1797, but again in 1799, 1800 and 1801. Early in 1803 the regiment was once again embodied and on 17 May was ordered to march for Windsor. Pleased with the regiment upon its appearance at Little Park, Windsor in the following year, the King announced that in future 'They shall be called my own.' Prior to this, the Staffordshire Militia had worn scarlet jackets with yellow facings, but now the King's Own Staffordshire Militia would wear scarlet with blue. The officers at the same time were entitled to assume the device of the round tower at Windsor Castle on their accoutrements. In 1881, when The King's Own became the 3rd and 4th Battalions of the South Staffordshire Regiment, the device was taken into use by officers of the regular battalions on their waist-belt clasps.

Colonel Cook also mentions the volunteers and recalls that when helmets were adopted the centre of that worn by the 4th Admin

Illustrations

382 The post-1881 officers' helmet plate. (*Bruce Bassett-Powell and Bon Bennet*)

383 An original watercolour painting by Harry Payne showing a private of the regiment, the centre of his helmet plate clearly showing the Sphinx. (*Anne SK Brown Military Collection, Brown University Library*)

Battalion (later 4th Staffordshire RVC, later 3rd VB) was a plain Stafford Knot with '4th A.B. Staffordshire Rifle Volunteers' inscribed on the Garter. The 3rd Admin Battalion (later 1st Staffordshire RVC, later 1st VB) had a bugle horn. Regarding the post-1881 volunteer battalions, Colonel Cook records that the Stafford Knot was used as a helmet plate centre piece.

South Wales Borderers
Late 24th (2nd Warwickshire) Regiment

Dress Regulations, 1883, 1891, 1894, 1900, 1904, 1911

On Helmet Plates: In silver, on a black velvet ground, the Welsh Dragon, within a laurel wreath. On the universal scroll 'The South Wales Borderers.'

In commemoration of the regiment's service during the Egyptian campaign of 1801, the Sphinx superscribed 'Egypt' was authorized as a badge in July of the following year. Well known are the 24th's encounters with the Zulu nation in 1879, the disaster at Isandlwana which was followed by the heroic stand at Rorke's Drift. After Isandlwana both Lieutenant's Melville and Coghill would sacrifice their lives in an attempt to save the Queen's Colour from the enemy. At first, the Colour was lost in the Buffalo River, but when found a few days later it was taken back to England where Queen Victoria asked to see it. Touched by the gallantry of the officers (both posthumously awarded Victoria Crosses), and the regiment's heroic stand at Rorke's Drift she placed a silver wreath of immortelles on the staff. A representation of the wreath would later become a feature of regimental badges. The pre-1881 officers' helmet plate had in silver, the Sphinx above Egypt with the Roman numerals XXIV below on a black velvet ground. Other ranks helmet plate centres has the Welsh Dragon, the circle reading 'South Wales Borderers'.

The regiment had five volunteer battalion. The 1st from Brecknockshire was photographed wearing home service helmets and author Bryn Owen, in his *History of the Welsh Militia & Volunteer Corps 1757-1908* series, includes three photographs of the 5th Volunteer Battalion. Two dated 1897, a third 1900, all show helmets with star plates being worn.

Illustrations

384 The officers' pre-1881 helmet plate.

385 The post-1881 queen's crown officers' helmet plate. (*Bruce Bassett-Powell and Bob Bennet*)

386 King's crown officers' helmet plate.

387 Other ranks helmet plate centre.

388 Colour plate after Frank Feller used for the frontispiece of Volume II of *Her Majesty's Army* by Walter Richards.

389 The 1st Brecknockshire Rifle Volunteer Corps was re-designated as 1st Volunteer Battalion South Wale Borderers in 1885. The illustration shows three members of the battalion wearing scarlet tunics with white facing, blue helmets with white metal star plates.

390 A fine example of an officer's helmet.

Suffolk Regiment

Late 12th (East Suffolk) Regiment

Dress Regulation, 1883, 1891. 1894, 1900, 1904, 1911

On Helmet Plates: In silver, on a black velvet ground, the Castle and Key, with scroll above inscribed 'Gibraltar', and scroll below inscribed Montis Insignia Calpe. On the universal scroll 'The Suffolk Regiment.'

For its services during the siege of 1779-83 the 12th was awarded, as a badge, the Castle of Gibraltar together with Key and motto *Montis insignia calpe* (Badge of the Rock of Gibraltar). The pre-1881 officers' star pattern helmet plate is illustrated and described on page 111 of *Head-dress Badges of the British Army* (Volume One) by Arthur L Kipling and Hugh L King: 'On a red velvet ground the Castle and Key in silver. Above the Garter a silver scroll inscribed *Gibraltar* and below the Garter a silver scroll inscribed *Montis Insignia Calpe*.' The other ranks helmet plate centres were all inscribed 'Suffolk' on the circle and also underwent the same change from two to three towers on the Castle.

Volume 15 (1936) of the *Journal of the Society for Army Historical Research* includes an article dealing with the badges worn by the several regiments of English militia. Written by Major HG Parkyn, the Cambridgeshire Militia are noted as having a representation of the Castle from the arms of the City of Cambridge in the centre of the helmet plate of 1878-81. In 1881, the regiment had provided the 4th Battalion of the Suffolk Regiment. A 3rd Battalion came from the West Suffolk Militia and Kipling and King mention a helmet plate with the following description: 'An eight-pointed star, the topmost point displaced by a Victorian crown. On this a laurel-wreath and within this the Garter. In the centre a castle. Below the Garter a three-part scroll inscribed *West Suffolk Militia*.'

Military Historical Society editor Gary Gibbs includes in his 'Badge Notes' section of *The Bulletin* for August 2015 (No 261) a Maltese Cross helmet plate to the 1st Suffolk Rifle Volunteers. With king's crown, the plate is described as, '…a brass badge blackened or bronzed, stamped out in one piece of metal.'

Of the usual design, with a lion between each arm of the cross, a stringed bugle appears in the center of a circle inscribed '1st Suffolk Rifle Volunteers'. The same item also shows an officer's Victorian plate to the 1st Volunteer Battalion. Of the universal star type, it appears as illustration 391, save that is in white metal and has an additional lower title scroll.

Illustrations

391 The officers' helmet plate as described in Dress Regulations. As we can see, the Castle is depicted with just two towers. On 30 January 1900, a War Office instruction directed that the Castle should in future be shown with three towers and in accordance with this a new version of the helmet plate subsequently appeared. (*Bruce Bassett-Powell and Bob Bennet*)

392 The officers' helmet plate with three towers. (Bruce Bassett-Powell, Bob Bennet)

393 PW Reynolds' colour plate from Colonel EAH Webb's 1914 history of the Suffolk Regiment is dated 1913 and shows an officer wearing the home service helmet and both the Queen's and King's Medals for South Africa.

394 The Suffolk Regiment had four volunteer battalions, the 1st at Ipswich, 2nd at Bury St Edmunds and 3rd, Cambridge. The 4th was located at Cambridge University and illustration 394 shows a private, officer and sergeant wearing grey helmets.

395 A star plate, with a Gibraltar Castle centre, was worn on the dark green helmets of the 1st Volunteer Battalion, and another by the 2nd who wore grey.

396 From Volume One of *Head-dress Badges of the British Army* by Arthur L Kipling and Hugh L King. Item '1811' is described by the authors as follows: 'An eight-pointed star, the topmost point displaced by a Victorian crown. On the star a shield bearing the Arms of Cambridge University surmounted by the monogram CUR. Below the Arms a scroll inscribed Universitas Cantabregiensis. In white metal.' Items '1814' and '1815' are blue cloth helmet plates (Queen's and King's crowns) of the 1st Cambridgeshire Rifle Volunteer Corps which under General Order 181 of December 1887 was re-designated as 3rd (Cambridgeshire) Volunteer Battalion Suffolk Regiment. Note how the post-1901 king's crown version has retained its rifle volunteer corps designation on the circle.

Welsh Regiment

Late 41st (The Welch) and 69th (South Lincolnshire) Regiments

Dress Regulations, 1883, 1891, 1894

On Helmet Plates: In silver on a black velvet ground, the Prince of Wales's Plume, with scroll below inscribed Gwell angau na Chywilydd. On the universal scroll 'The Welsh Regiment.'

Dress Regulations, 1900, 1904, 1911

On Helmet Plates: In silver on a black velvet ground, the Prince of Wales's Plume, with scroll below inscribed Gwell angau na Chywilydd. The coronet in gilt or gilding metal. On the universal scroll 'The Welsh Regiment.'

The Prince of Wales's Plumes, Coronet and motto were authorised for the 41st Regiment in December 1831 at the same time as the motto, *Gwell angau na Chywilydd (Death rather than Dishonour)*. The Plumes, etc, appeared on a red velvet ground in the centre of the officers' pre 1881 helmet plates. Below this was the number '41' in silver. Other ranks post-1881 helmet plate centres had the Prince of Wales insignia and the motto *Gwell angau na Chywilydd,* the circles reading 'The Welsh'.

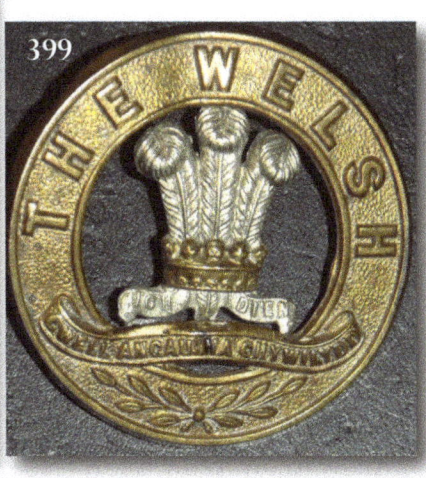

105

Author Bryn Owen records in his book, *Glamorgan Regiments of Militia,* how at Cowshot Camp, in 1897, the other ranks were issued with new home service blue cloth helmets to replace the shakos hitherto worn. The Royal Glamorgan Militia had provided the regiment's 3rd Battalion in 1881.

Illustrations

397 An other ranks pre-1881 helmet complete with plate showing the detachable '69' centre.

398 The officers' post-1881 helmet plate with gilt coronet. (*Bruce Bassett-Powell and Bob Bennet*)

399 An example of the other ranks helmet plate centre. Note how the motto scroll extends onto the circle.

400 The original artwork provided by artist Edgar Holloway for one of Gale & Polden's postcard series. (*Anne SK Brown Military Collection, Brown University Library*)

401 From a photograph taken by WM Crockett of Plymouth, illustration 401 shows Sergeant Drummer McKelvey of the 1st Battalion with the regimental goat.

402 Major George Frederick Heyworth, formerly of the 5th Dragoon Guards, who served with the Glamorgan Militia from 1869 to 1884. The helmet plate is of the universal crowned star type, in silver, with the cypher 'VR' in the centre of a circle inscribed 'Royal Glamorgan Light Infy.'

403 The helmet plate being worn in illustration 402. Bryn Owen also describes, and illustrates, another officer's plate of the same type, but with the addition of a stringed bugle horn below the circle. Helmet plates for the period 1881-1908, records Bryn Owen, were for both officers and other ranks as worn by the regulars of the Welsh Regiment.

Worcestershire Regiment

Late 29th (Worcestershire) and 36th (Herefordshire) Regiments

Dress Regulations, 1883

On Helmet Plates: On a black velvet ground, a silver eight-pointed star. In gilt metal, within a silver circle on the star, a Castle on a raised ground of blue enamel. On the star, at the bottom, a scroll in gilt metal, inscribed 'Firm.' On the universal scroll, in gilt letters, 'The Worcestershire Regiment.'

Dress Regulations, 1891, 1894

On Helmet Plates: On a black velvet ground, a silver eight-pointed star. On the star, in gilt metal, the Garter with motto. Within the Garter, in silver the Lion, pierced on a black velvet ground. Below the Garter, in gilt metal, a scroll inscribed 'Firm.'

Dress Regulations, 1900, 1904, 1911

On Helmet Plates: On a black velvet ground, a silver eight-pointed star. On the star, in gilt or gilding metal, the Garter with motto. Within the Garter, the Lion in silver on a black velvet ground. Below the Garter, a scroll in gilt or gilding metal, inscribed 'Firm.' On the universal scroll 'The Worcestershire Regiment.'

A watercolour by Richard Simkin of an officer c1842 shows a jacket being adorned with gold lace and an oblong silver and gilt shoulder-belt plate which features in its centre a lion. This is the ancient badge of the regiment, its star device only originating from 1784 when pouch badges were discontinued. Through the influence of Queen Charlotte, the 29th were permitted to continue wearing star plates on their valises. Official authority was obtained in May 1838. Major T J Edwards, in his book *Military Customs,* relates the star badge to the fact that founder of the regiment, Thomas Farrington, was a colonel of the Coldstream Guards and that this was also the origin of the nickname Guards of the Line. Seen on many badges and devices, the motto *Firm* certainly dates from 1773, if not before.

Thanks to the late RW Bennett, and his 1994 book *Badges of the Worcestershire Regiment,* we have a comprehensive and well-illustrated account of the helmet plates worn. For both the 29th and 36th Regiments he shows officers' star helmet plates displaying the relevant numbers, but without regimental badges. The 36th, however, has a small silver scroll just below the Garter inscribed 'Firm'. Both plates are in gilt metal, the '29' being on a black leather ground, '36' set on black velvet.

RW Bennett tells how the post-1881 helmet plate was designed by Militia adjutant, Captain R Holden. Here was the star of the 29th, 'Firm' from the 36th and a castle, an old badge of the Worcester Militia which had provided the 3rd and 4th Battalions in 1881. This indeed is the plate described in Dress Regulations for 1883. An amendment issued in the same year, however, would order the blue enamel behind the castle to be replaced by silver.

The pattern for the other ranks gilding metal universal star helmet plate was sealed on 8 February 1882 and showed the star and castle in the centre of a circle inscribed 'Worcester' and, replacing the usual laurel spray, the word 'Firm'. It would seem that the shape of the star used was not popular and subsequently a replacement plate was designed and sealed on 23 November 1883.

Returning to the officers' helmet plates, RW Bennett tells how the former 29th Regiment (now 1st Battalion Worcestershire Regiment) had objected to the use of the castle in the centre of the plates and suggested that their lion badge be used instead. The proposal was agreed to and subsequently the lion device, within a gilt Garter, was granted by Horse Guards letter of 17 October 1890. The other ranks plates were also changed, the pattern being sealed on 16 August 1891.

407

408

409

410

412

Roger Bennett includes an interesting photograph in his book of a group of Worcestershire Militia officers, c1880, wearing both the home service helmet and its shako predecessor. A specimen of the officers' helmet plate is illustrated, and this is described as: 'Silver universal pattern with tower on a black velvet ground in the centre of the Garter.' Below this is a wide scroll inscribed 'Worcester'.

Black pears have been associated with Worcester since Roman times and representations of these would find their way to the city's seals and coats of arms. The several rifle volunteer companies raised from 1859 would bear this tradition in mind when designing their insignia. There is a note in the clothing records of the 14th Worcestershire Rifle Volunteer Corps, raised in Worcester in 1860, that helmets were received in November 1880.

The existing rifle volunteer companies were, in 1880, merged into two battalions, the 1st with headquarters at Hagley, the 2nd at Worcester. Both wore green uniforms. Roger Bennett explains that, 'Initially, both battalions adopted a Maltese cross type of plate, in white metal for officers and staff-sergeants and blackened brass for other ranks.' He goes on to say that 'The officers' pattern was often blackened, and then the highlights polished silver.' He also notes that as there were two styles of inscription, it is possible that no less than twelve varieties may have existed. Four volunteer plates are illustrated, all of the Maltese Cross type, all with a representation of a pear tree in the centre. Wording on the title circles noted are: '1st Battn Worcestershire R.V', '1st Worcestershire Rifle Volunteers', '1st

411

Worcestershire Rifle Volunteer Corps', '2nd Battn Worcestershire R.V' and '2nd Worcestershire Rifle Volunteers'.

In 1883, the 1st and 2nd Worcestershire Rifle Volunteer Corps were re-designated respectively as 1st and 2nd Volunteer Battalions Worcestershire Regiment. For the 2nd Volunteer Battalion, Roger Bennet illustrates an officer's Victorian crown plate which has the castle device in the centre and an additional scroll reading, '2nd Volunteer Battalion'. The other ranks version is also shown, the wording on the circle being, '2nd Volr. Batt. Worcestershire'. Come the smaller star, and appearance of the lion, both officers' and other ranks plates followed suit.

Notes referring to the helmet plates worn by the volunteer battalions refer to them retaining the Maltese Cross type well into the 1880s. Roger Bennett mentions a photograph taken at the unveiling of Queen Victoria's statue at Worcester which shows a number of volunteer officers, some with star pattern helmet plates, other with the Maltese Cross. It is thought that the 1st Volunteer Battalion, who retained their rifle-style uniforms, retained their plates until replacing the helmet with the busby in the early 1890s. Back in 1992 I was privileged to provide for the Military Historical Society their 'Special Number' for that year. It was titled *The Volunteer Infantry 1880-1908* and included a photograph loaned to me by the Worcestershire Regimental Museum. It showed a group from the 2nd Volunteer Battalion on the occasion of them having received their Volunteer Long Service Medals in 1895. All are in rifle-style uniform with star plates on the helmets.

Illustrations

404 Officer's queen's crown helmet plate with castle centre. (*Bruce Bassett-Powell and Bob Bennet*)

405 Other ranks helmet plate centre with castle and large star centre.

406 Other ranks helmet with castle and small star centre.

407 Officers' helmet plate with lion centre. (*Bruce Bassett-Powell and Bob Bennet*)

408 Other ranks helmet plate with lion centre.

409 Officers' king's crown helmet.

410 Shortly after war had been declared in 1914, the Aldershot firm of Gale & Polden commissioned several leading military artists to produce artwork for postcards featuring British regiments. In sets of six, the cards showed scenes in France, as well as officers and men in full dress uniforms. There can be no doubt as to the time in this image by Edgar Holloway, the message on the newsboys' evening news banner offering the latest war news being clear. Led by the drum major, out from the barracks march the battalion, the chin straps of their helmets fastened via hooks at the back. Only the sentry, who is seen presenting arms, has his smartly placed under his chin. (*Anne SK Brown Military Collection, Brown University Library*)

411 A second card in the above set shows two officers chatting, 'Firm' being clearly seen on the Regimental Colour. (*Anne SK Brown Military Collection, Brown University Library*)

412 Officer's helmet plate, 29th Regiment.

York and Lancaster Regiment

Late 65th (2nd Yorkshire North Riding) and 84th Regiments

Dress Regulations, 1883, 1891, 1894, 1900, 1904, 1911

On Helmet Plates: In silver and gilt metal, on a black velvet ground, the Union Rose. On the universal scroll, 'The York & Lancaster Regiment.'

The Union Rose was an old badge of the 84th Regiment and appeared on the pre-1881 officers' helmet

plates together with the number. The 65th had been awarded the badge of a Royal Tiger commemorating its services in India for the period 1796 to 1819 and this appeared above a chevron inscribed *India-Arabia* on the regiment's first helmet plates, but not used after 1881. Other than queen's and king's crowns, there would be no change in the design of the officers' post-1881 plate. The other ranks helmet plate centres had 'York & Lancaster' on the circles and the rose in gilding and white metals in the centre.

The 2nd and 8th Yorkshire (West Riding) Rifle Volunteer Corps joined the regiment in 1881. With headquarters in Sheffield, the 2nd Corps

was re-designated in February 1883 as the 1st (Hallamshire) Volunteer Battalion—Hallamshire being the name given to the southernmost part of the West Riding of Yorkshire, the centre of which is the great steel city of Sheffield. Part of Sheffield's coat of arms is a collection of eight arrows to illustrate Sheffield's 'piercing' trade (recognised worldwide was its production of knives) and it was this device that the 2nd Yorkshire (West Riding) RVC took as a badge. Dixon Pickup, in his book *West York Rifle Volunteers 1859-1887* shows an other ranks white metal helmet plate with the arrows in the centre of a strap inscribed '2nd West York (Hallamshire) Rifles'. An example of a post-1883 officer's plate can be seen in an article by Ernest J Martin published by the Military Historical Society (*The Bulletin* No 20) in May 1955. Of the universal type, the plate has a gilt rose in the centre of the Garter and a second scroll inscribed '1st Hallamshire Volr Battn.'

The Castle Museum at York has an officer's helmet plate to the 8th Yorkshire (West Riding) Rifle Volunteer Corps which is silver plated with a bugle on a black enamel ground in the centre of a strap inscribed '8th West Riding of Yorkshire Vols.' Dixon Pickup illustrates the other ranks version which also has the bugle central device. Plates with the 2nd Volunteer Battalion designation followed, a particularly fine example those worn by officers turning up recently in auction.

Illustrations

413 An officer's Victorian crown helmet plate with gilt and silver Union Rose and silver title scroll 'The York & Lancaster Regiment'. (*Bruce Bassett-Powell and Bob Bennet*)

414 Other ranks helmet plate centre.

415 Supplement No 94 in Richard Simkin's 'Military Types' series produced for the Army and Navy Gazette. Published on 5 October 1895, the artist's painting seems to have been set just outside of what could be the officers' mess on some home station. The 1st Battalion York and Lancaster Regiment at time of publication were in Ireland. In the distance a squad lined up in two ranks is being addressed by an NCO. They stand to attention, their rifles at their sides. Unconcerned with what is going on, two officers seemingly pose for the artist. Standing, one is wearing his full dress tunic and home service helmet, the officer seated wears a frock jacket and forage cap which displays both the royal tiger and rose.

416 An original watercolour by Harry Payne which shows a sentry standing at ease with his bayonet fixed. He wears a king's crown helmet plate, gilding and white metal rose and tiger collar badges and Y&L brass shoulder titles. Just turning a corner, a bugler. (*Anne SK Brown Military Collection, Brown University Library*)

417 An original watercolour by J McNeill of a corporal who wears a king's crown helmet plate. The artist has given him both the Queen's and King's Medals for South Africa. (*Anne SK Brown Military Collection, Brown University Library*)

418 'March Past', a Gale & Polden postcard after Ernest Ibbetson.

419 Officer's, king's crown, helmet plate to the 2nd Volunteer Battalion.

BIBLIOGRAPHY

Army Museums Ogilby Trust: *Index to British Military Costume Prints 1500-1914,* 1972.

Bennett, RW: *Badges of the Worcestershire Regiment,* published by the author in 1994.

Brinson, Daniel: *Military Insignia of Gloucestershire,* Covithick, 2009.

Carman, WY: *Richard Simkin's Uniforms of the British Army – The Infantry Regiments,* Webb & Bower, Exeter, 1985.

Edwards, Major TJ: *Military Customs,* Gale & Polden, Aldershot, 1954.

Grierson, Lieutenant-General Sir James Moncrieff: *Records of the Scottish Volunteer Force 1859-1908,* William Blackwood & Sons, 1909.

Harris, RG: *The Irish Regiments A Pictorial History 1683-1987,* Spellmount, 1989.

Ival, D Endean and Thomas, Charles: *Military Insignia of Cornwall,* Penwith Books, 1974.

Kipling, Arthur L and King, Hugh L: *Head-dress Badges of the British Army, Volume 1,* Frederick Muller Ltd, London, 1978.

Military Historical Society: *The Bulletin,* Nos 1 to date.

Owen, Bryn: 'The History of the Welsh Militia and Volunteer Corps', Palace Books Ltd, Caernarfon. Several volumes dating from 1989 to 2000

Pickup, KD: *West York Rifle Volunteers,* published by the author.

Richards, Walter: *Her Majesty's Army,* Virtue & Co, London, 1890s.

Richards, Walter: *His Majesty's Territorial Army,* Virtue & Co, London, 1911/10.

Sainsbury, JD: *Hertfordshire Soldiers From 1757,* Hertfordshire Local History Council, 1969.

Society for Army Historical Research: Numerous volumes, 1921 to date.

War Office: The Army List, several editions between 1859 and 1914.

War Office: Dress Regulations for 1883, 1891, 1894, 1900, 1904 and 1911.

Westlake, Ray and Litchfield, Norman: *The Volunteer Artillery 1859-1908,* Sherwood Press, 1982.

Westlake, Ray: *Royal Engineers (Volunteers) 1859-1908,* Sherwood Press, 1883.

Westlake, Ray: *The Territorial Battalions: A Pictorial History 1859-1895,* Spellmount, 1986.

Westlake, Ray: *English and Welsh Infantry Regiments: An Illustrated Record of Service 1662-1994,* Spellmount, 1995.

Westlake, Ray: *Tracing the Rifle Volunteers,* Pen & Sword, Barnsley, 2010.

Westlake, Ray: *A Guide to the Volunteers of England 1859-1908,* Naval & Military Press, 2019.

Westlake, Ray: *A Guide to the Civic Heraldry of England,* Naval & Military Press, 2019.

In addition to the above, several regimental histories have been consulted.

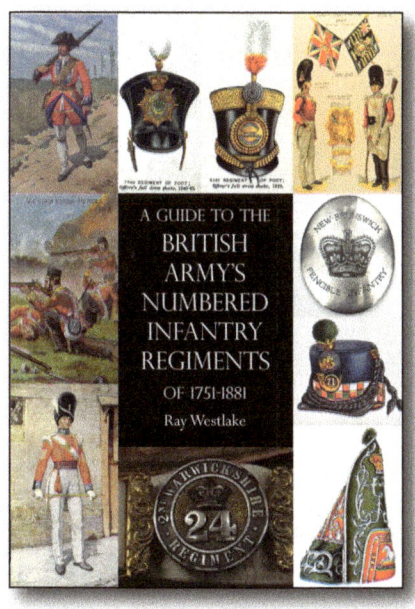
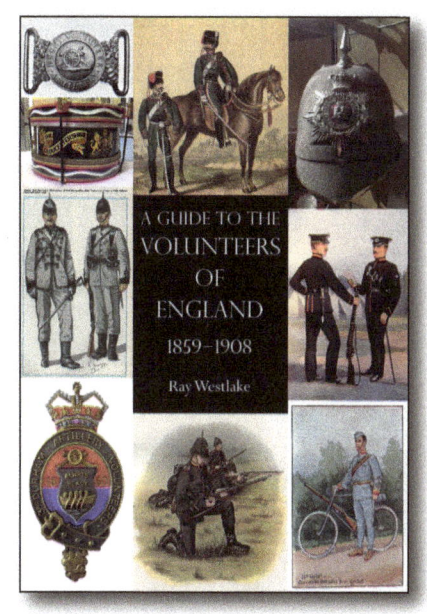

RAY WESTLAKE'S GUIDES TO THE BRITISH ARMY

A Series of British Army Reference Books

New "Westlake" classics!

Ray's series of British Army 'Guides' fill an important gap by placing succinct information on the subject matter in an accessible manner.

FULL COLOUR ILLUSTRATIONS THROUGHOUT EACH VOLUME

www.naval-military-press.com

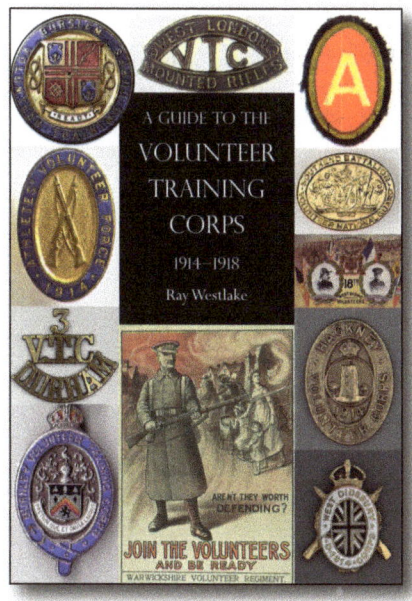
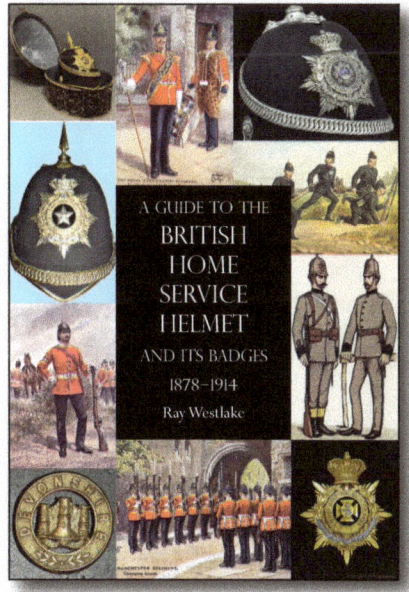
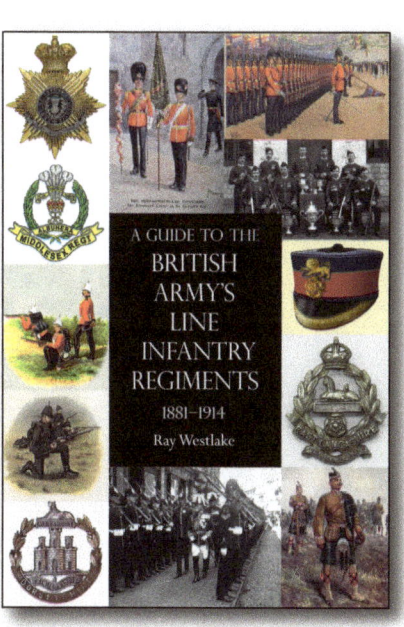

HER MAJESTY'S ARMY 1888

A descriptive account of the various regiments now comprising the Queen's Forces & Indian and Colonial Forces

This is a much sought-after three-volume set – the first two are devoted entirely to the British Army, with the third to India and the Colonies, all from their first establishment to the 'present time', c.1888. The author's main aim was to describe the organisation and condition of each unit as it was in the 1880s.

Consisting of written sketches of the various regiments, they contain much useful information on their battles, campaigns and prior fighting achievements, complemented **with 41 excellent, full-page chromolithographic uniform plates**.

The plates in the first two volumes are by G.D. Giles who saw service with the British Army in India, Afghanistan and Egypt; those of the Indian and Colonial forces volume are by H. Bunnett. This work was originally published c.1888 by J.S. Virtue & Co Ltd, a London publishing business, the main feature of which was the production of illustrated works.

**Softback edition in 3 volumes
1210 pages in total +
41 colour uniform plates
printed on 70lbs paper
Product code: 28703**

**Hardback edition in 3 volumes
1210 pages in total +
41 colour uniform plates
printed on 70lbs paper
Product code: 28703HB**

HEAD-DRESS BADGES OF THE BRITISH ARMY VOL 1. 1800-1918
ISBN 9781843425120

Illustrated record of badges worn on every type of head-dress from the mitre cap to the Shako to the Field Service cap, with detailed comments. Changes in regimental title and dates of amalgamations given. Starts in the year 1800.

HEAD-DRESS BADGES OF THE BRITISH ARMY VOL 2. 1919-1979
ISBN 9781843425137

From end of the Great War to 1979. Includes OTC badges and all special units raised in WWII as well as those of the Gurkha regiments.

Following the death of Hugh King and the disposal of his collection by auction. The Naval and Military Press reissued both volumes of his and L Kipling's work. First published in the seventies they still remain the bible for all serious badge collectors. Intended as the standard reference, these two volumes are a record of badges worn on every type of head-dress from the mitre cap to the Shako to the Field Service cap, with complete with detailed comments and identifier photographs. Changes in regimental title and dates of amalgamations given.

It should be noted that dealers and auctioneers refer to Kipling and King numbers for identification purposes.

www.ingramcontent.com/pod-product-compliance
Lightning Source LLC
Chambersburg PA
CBHW061543010526
44113CB00023B/2779